CHURCH IN HISTORY SERIES

The Church in the Age of Orthodoxy and the Enlightenment

Consolidation and Challenge from 1600 to 1800

ROBERT G. CLOUSE

Publishing House
St. Louis

Concordia Publishing House, St. Louis, Missouri
Copyright © 1980 Concordia Publishing House
ISBN: 0-570-06273-X

MANUFACTURED IN THE UNITED STATES OF AMERICA

Library of Congress Cataloging in Publication Data

Clouse, Robert G 1931-
     The church in the age of Orthodoxy and the Enlightenment.

     (Church in history series; v. 5)
     Includes index.
     1. Church history—17th century. 2. Church history—18th century.
I. Title. II. Series.
BR440.C57   282′.09′03   79-17381
ISBN 0-570-06273-X

Contents

Introduction

This book is a survey of Christian history 1600—1800. These two centuries were characterized by a shift toward a more secular outlook in Western thought generally. Beginning with the post-Reformation emphasis on orthodoxy and extending through the rise of modern science, this period culminated in attempts to apply the scientific outlook to society during the 18th-century revolutions. Though some Christian leaders of this period (e.g., Johann Gerhard, Philipp Jacob Spener, and John Wesley) are not as well known as some leaders of preceding ages (e.g., Augustine, Martin Luther, and John Calvin), many thought patterns and movements surfaced, and many problems developed that have continued into our time.

The modern state system grew during the two centuries from 1600 to 1800. The last important European religious conflict, the Thirty Years' War, saw a shift in loyalty from religion to politics and became in essence the "first world war." When the struggle ended in 1648 with the Peace of Westphalia, absolute dynastic monarchies were clearly to be the supreme institutions in western Europe. The state became more important than religion as a focus for the loyalty of its citizens. In France and certain areas of the Holy Roman Empire this led to a decline in religious toleration; in the Reformed states of the Netherlands and in England there was more freedom. At first glance the shift away from bitter religious struggles to a more secular approach might be viewed as a wholly positive step, but, with the advent of the American and French revolutions of the 18th century, society was faced with a new source of bigotry and intolerance, namely, the nation-state.

Another problem left over for the 20th century is in the relation between science and Christianity. Though many early leaders of the scientific revolution were Christians, tensions soon developed between religious faith and the quest for understanding the natural world. As a result, many early scientists were persecuted by church organizations, and the writings of the Enlightenment, which defended and popularized science, attacked Christianity. The most famous of the early martyrs for the cause of natural science was Galileo. His *Dialogo . . . sopra i due massimi sistemi del mondo . . . (Dialog on the Two Chief World Systems,* 1632), which defended the new heliocentric cosmology and made the defenders of the medieval geocentric view appear ridiculous, led to quarrels between him and the Roman Catholic Church. The ensuing trial led to Galileo's recantation and the sentence that he spend the rest of his days under house arrest. Tension between faith and science was further increased by Voltaire, a leader of the Enlightenment, who defended science in such a way as to make it antagonistic to revealed religion. Certain churchmen tried to adapt their faith to the new science and espoused deism, but this did little to help the cause of the historic Christian faith.

Some tried to come to terms with the new scientific outlook by adjusting their faith; others, such as the Pietists and individuals like John and Charles Wesley and George Whitefield, emphasized a religion of experience. Their outlook represented as much a reaction against the intellectualism and dogmatism of Orthodoxy as did the Enlightenment. But instead of attacking Christian teaching they found new sources of strength within it—a fervent moralism, personal conversion, holiness of life, a concern for human need, and a devotional experience reflected in prayers and hymns. Pietism was a call for believers to manifest Christ in their daily lives. It tried to internalize religion rather than emphasize external formalities and creeds.

The 17th and 18th centuries also were a time of the expansion of Europe and the rise of Western civilization to a position of global leadership. From the 6th to the 16th centuries there were four major world cultures: India, the Middle East, China, and western Europe, all in relative balance. During certain periods one or the other dominated, but not as the West has done since the 16th century. Beginning with the voyages of exploration in the 15th and 16th centuries and continuing to the imperialism of the 19th and 20th centuries, Western civilization has overwhelmed the other cultures. Western political arrangements, technology, and science have developed a life-style copied by many world leaders. During the period covered by this book, Europeans colonized distant lands and engaged in much missionary activity. As a result, many natives in the colonies became Christians.

1.

Politics
and Ecclesiastical Polemics

THE POLITICAL SITUATION
IN THE 17TH CENTURY

In the early 17th century Europe was divided into several states whose relations were strained not only by dynastic ambitions but also by differences in religion. France, the Netherlands, and England controlled the Channel and the Atlantic approaches to the Baltic and North Seas.

France was potentially the strongest because of its large population and abundant resources. During the reigns of Henry IV (1553—1610; king of Navarre as Henry III 1572—89; king of France 1589—1610), Louis XIII (1601—43; king 1610—43), and the early years of the rule of Louis XIV (1638—1715; king 1643—1715) power had been consolidated with the king. The authority of the nobles was reduced, and royal agents secured throughout the land a measure of cooperation that laid the basis for the brilliant period of the reign of Louis XIV. Peace was secured with the French Protestants, the Huguenots, and under competent ministers like Richelieu (1585—1642; chief minister of Louis XIII 1624—42) and Mazarin (1602—61; succeeded Richelieu as prime minister) the country was rebuilt from damage done during the religious wars of the 16th century. As Spain declined, France became the leading Roman Catholic power of the 17th century.

England, though not as large as France, was influential because it was well organized. During the 16th century the

Tudor dynasty had reduced the English nobility to obedience, reorganized the government, worked closely with Parliament, and reformed the church. The Anglican Church, or Church of England, became a leader among Protestant bodies in the 17th century. The attempt of the first two Stuart kings, James I (1566—1625; king of Scotland as James VI 1567—1625; king of Great Britain 1603—25) and Charles I (1600—49; king 1625—49), to carry on Tudor policies led to civil war (1642—51). This Puritan Revolution, or Great Rebellion, caused England to develop differently than France.

After a long struggle with Spain, the Netherlands became one of the leading commercial and colonial powers. The government was unique, since each of the seven provinces that made up the United Netherlands had its own legislature and sent delegates to the States General to act on common problems. There was no king or prince in the Netherlands, but there was a stadtholder who could act as chief executive. Despite its limited size and population, the Dutch, because of wealth and commercial leadership, could compete with Spain, England, and France. Holland was a center for the exchange of merchandise of all sorts and for insurance, banking, and shipbuilding. The Netherlands became one of the early centers of Calvinism—in fact, Calvinism became the state religion. But later in the 17th century the state adopted a policy of toleration.

Two of the great powers of the 16th century, Spain and the Holy Roman Empire (in effect a German state), were declining during the 17th century. The crowns of Spain and of the Holy Roman Empire were united in the person of the Hapsburg heir, Charles V (1500—58; king of Spain as Charles I 1516—56; Holy Roman emperor 1519—56), who became the most powerful ruler of his age. A devout Catholic, he fought a losing struggle against Lutheranism. Upon his abdication he left his Spanish possessions to his son Philip II (1527—98; king of Spain 1556—98) and the Holy Roman Empire to his brother Ferdinand I (1503—64; Holy Roman emperor 1556—64). This permanently separated Spain and the Empire.

Philip made Spain the leading power of the Catholic or

Counter Reformation. All religious dissent was suppressed, commerce and industry were tightly controlled, and the military strength of Spain was committed against the Protestants and the French monarchy. Spanish policy led to rebellion in the Low Countries and to the disaster of the Armada in 1588. A series of defeats by the French in the later 16th century and in the 17th century completed the Spanish demoralization. Gone was the wealth that had produced beautiful palaces and cathedrals. The precious metal mines of the New World were exhausted and no longer able to supply the homeland with gold and silver. Castile, the most prosperous area of Spain, declined because of heavy taxes, poor government, depopulation, and ruined industry.

By the 16th century the Holy Roman Empire, which was intended to be the successor of the ancient Roman Empire, had become a loose federation of small German-speaking principalities that acknowledged the Hapsburgs as nominal rulers. The Empire never achieved the unity of France or England, and, because the emperors were Roman Catholics, the rise of Lutheranism and Calvinism increased its problems. The Thirty Years' War, which will be considered in detail later in this chapter, was an attempt to deal with the religious and political disunity of the Empire.

A third major area of Europe centers on the Baltic Sea and includes the states of eastern Europe and Scandinavia. The major 17th-century power in this part of the continent was Sweden. Though lacking resources and population, this Lutheran land, under able leaders, dominated the Baltic states of Europe with military force. Later in the century Russia challenged Swedish domination and in the 18th century became the leading Eastern power. The Russians traced their Eastern Orthodox faith to the early church councils and the apostles. In tension with both Roman Catholics and Protestants, the Russian Orthodox Church believed that with the fall of Constantinople (1453) the center of God's purpose had shifted to Moscow. According to this doctrine of the "third Rome," Russia became the guardian of the true faith until the return of Christ. The "true faith" consisted mainly of formalistic ritual usually ministered by illiterate priests to people who had only the most superficial acquaintance with the Christian message. Despite these limitations, Eastern Orthodoxy aided the Russian czars to consolidate and expand their control. These rulers increasingly took on the style and manners of the Byzantine autocrats of Constantinople. They reduced the older Slavic kingdoms of Poland and Lithuania to submission and moved Russian borders westward.

EUROPE, AMERICA, AND THE ORIENT

While dynastic and religious changes were taking place in 16th- and 17th-century Europe, the Christian faith was carried far abroad by colonists and missionaries. Beginning with the voyages of Columbus (1451—1506; first voyage 1492), explorers and adventurers laid claim to vast areas of the Americas for Spain and Portugal. The Spanish claimed the lion's share of the new hemisphere, including Mexico, Peru, Central America, and the West Indies, and established settlements in Colombia, Panama, California, New Mexico, Chile, and the area of the River Plate (*Rio de la Plata*). The expansions into America resembled early medieval missionary work in pagan Germany. Soldiers, called conquistadors, were accompanied by Roman Catholic missionaries who established churches and schools. Many of the troops that came to conquer such empires as the Aztec and the Incan were the scum of Spanish society, and they were often encouraged by fanaticism and a desire for plunder reminiscent of the worst of the medieval crusades. But the friars who came to preach and teach were often very noble. Among them was Bartolome de Las Casas (1474—1566). For over 40 years Las Casas preached to the Spanish that the Indians were human beings and should be treated with kindness and consideration. Toribio Alfonso de Mogrovejo y Robles (1538—1606), 2nd Archbishop of Lima, Peru (ca. 1578/80—1606), and called "Apostle of Peru," is said to have confirmed many hundreds of thousands. Mass baptisms resulted in "converts" who had very little knowledge of Christianity.

In an attempt to deal with problems caused by contact between Indians and Europeans, separate villages were established for Christian Indians. These "reductions" were a Roman Catholic form of the later reservations established by the United States. In Brazil, Peru, Mexico, and Paraguay these settlements offered the Indians a better way of life. By the early 17th century in Paraguay, for example, there were 30 clerical estates or reductions, each with a church, hospital, convent, and a school where the brightest children could learn Latin. Governed by clerics, these communities offered their residents an eight-hour workday, compulsory divine services, and various recreational activities.

Most of the Indians of South and Central America did not live on reservations but attended parish churches modeled after those of Spain and Portugal. Under control of distant bishops, these churches remained untouched by the Counter Reformation. As a result, the medieval church enjoyed an Indian summer, so to say, in the New World.

As the Spaniards led the way in evangelizing the Americas, the Portuguese expanded in the Orient. Though they encountered more advanced civilizations and stronger religions than those in the New World, the Portuguese brought civil control and Christianity to Goa, Malacca, and Macao. By 1620 the Spanish had an archbishop, a Dominican university, and 2,000 baptized converts in the Philippines. Roman Catholic successes here raised expectations among the missionaries that other victories would follow.

Francis Xavier (1506—52), one of the founders of the Society of Jesus (Jesuits), was appointed papal representative to the East Indies. He arrived at Goa in 1542 and later went to Malacca and Japan. Before he was forced to leave Japan he had established a Christian community of over 2,000 members. He died while trying to enter China. Though he mastered none of the languages he encountered, he felt at home among Hindus, Muslims, and Buddhists. He appealed to the masses. Working under protection of the government, he gathered people by ringing a handbell. Then, speaking through interpreters, he recited the Apostles' Creed, the Ten Commandments, the Hail Mary, and the Lord's Prayer. After weeks or months of this, he baptized those who had memorized these statements and professed faith in God. He then moved on to another place but left some followers behind to carry on the work.

Christian missionaries in the Orient faced strong competing religions. Often they found that Christian worship was welcome in the temples, but that Hindu and Buddhist rites would continue to be observed. The traditional attitude of Christians had been that idols must be destroyed and non-Christian worship suppressed. But in India and China this exclusive outlook was modified as a result of the toleration, holiness, and asceticism of the Asian religions. In the policy of accommodation, as it came to be called, the Jesuits led the way with a gentle approach to the beliefs and traditions of Asia, holding that such procedure would aid the presentation of the Gospel. They tried to sort out the customs of the Japanese, Chinese, or Indians and determine which were merely social and civil and which were incompatible with Christianity. The Italians Matteo Ricci (1552—1610) and Robert(o) de Nobili (1577—1656) were among the better known Jesuit exponents of missionary adaptation.

Trained in science at the Roman College, Ricci spent the years 1572—82 at Goa and Cochin before going to China. In typical evangelistic fashion he began his work by showing clocks, astronomical instruments, maps, and books. He then spent hours in discussion on the agreement between Confucianism and Christianity. Hundreds of thousands of copies of his dialog between a Chinese scholar and a European priest were distributed to the Chinese. By the year of his death there were over 2,000 Christians in China. As the 17th century progressed, the work of adaptation to ancient custom begun by Ricci was undermined and destroyed as a result of the "affair of the rites." In a series of decisions the papacy declared that it was wrong to value the Confucian tradition too highly and to pay undue reverence to one's ancestors. The Chinese emperor was upset by what he regarded as an insult to the customs of his people and forced Christian missions from his country.

Nobili was a nephew of Cardinal Bellarmine and related to Pope Julius III. He was sent as missionary to India in 1604, arrived in Goa in 1605, and worked especially in Madura. He dressed and lived like a sannyasi (Hindu ascetic). The Christian community that resulted from his work is said to have numbered over 100,000.

Japan seemed to offer an opportunity to repeat the success that Christian missionaries had enjoyed in the Philippines. By 1614 there were at least 300,000 Christians in Japan. The rapid conversion to Christianity was halted by fear that the priests would help the Westerners to take over the government. In a series of horrible persecutions marked by savage tortures the Christian church in Japan was destroyed. A decree of 1638 closed the land to foreigners, and by the end of the century few Christians were left in Japan. The fate of the Japanese church illustrates the problems of early Christian missions in the Orient. Despite impressive initial gains, the work of winning south and east Asia to Christ did not prosper as did similar efforts in the Americas. The Philippines are the only Roman Catholic land in east Asia.

ARMINIAN VERSUS REFORMED

At the same time that missionaries were carrying the Gospel far abroad, their fellow churchmen in Europe were trying to define Christianity precisely. Doctrinal quarrels were often intertwined with political struggles and led to conflict between various groups such as Arminians and Reformed (Calvinists),[1] Lutherans and Reformed, and Roman Catholics and Protestants. The conflict between the Arminians and the strict Calvinists centered in the Netherlands. The Arminian party was named for Jacobus Arminius (1560—1609), a Dutch theologian who was trained at Leiden and Geneva before he became pastor at Amsterdam. The Calvinist theology of

Arminius' day had been developed from the view of its founder, John Calvin (1509—64), by Theodore Beza (1519—1605) and other leaders of the Reformed scholastic movement. These men emphasized Biblical literalism (the tendency to adopt literal interpretations), predestination, and presbyterian church government. Arminius, reacting against this rigid system, proclaimed that God's offer of grace was universal and that individuals possessed the freedom to respond to God in faith.

In 1603 Arminius was called to the position of professor of theology at the University of Leiden despite the protest of Franciscus Gomarus (originally Gommer; 1563—1641), a professor at the school. A controversy between Arminius and Gomarus focused on the precise meaning of predestination. The conflict led Arminius to state in an even clearer manner his opposition to certain aspects of Calvin's theology. He felt that Calvin made God the author of sin and denied genuine freedom to human beings. Gomarus tried to counter these views. The bitter debate that resulted led to a division in the ranks of the Reformed Church. Arminius tried to bring the two sides together. He asked the estates of Holland and West Friesland to call a national synod to deal with the matter. In 1609 he appeared before the States General of the United Netherlands and explained his ideas. But he died before the meeting ended.

After the death of Arminius his followers continued to spread his teachings. In 1610 they issued a document called Remonstrance, which, in the course of a plea for toleration, stated the five major points of Arminianism: (1) The eternal decree of salvation refers to those who believe and persevere in the faith; (2) Christ died for all; (3) One can do nothing truly good until born again by the Holy Spirit; (4) Grace is not irresistible; (5) One can fall from grace. Many in the Netherlands, including theologians such as Simon Episcopius (1583—1643) and Jan Uytenbogaert (1557—1644), statesmen like Jan van Oldenbarneveldt (1547—1619), and even the leading scholar of the day, Hugo Grotius (1583—1645), joined the Arminian cause.

The 1618—19 Synod of Dordrecht was convened to settle

the Arminian Controversy. Invitations were sent to all Calvinist churches of Europe, and 27 of the more than 100 delegates at the meeting were from such places as Germany, Switzerland, England, and Scotland. The Arminians, or Remonstrants, as they were often called, were condemned in a fivefold series of decrees that refuted the statement of 1610 point by point. These decrees defined the classic Calvinist faith as teaching total depravity, unconditional election, limited atonement, irresistible grace, and the perseverance absolute of the saints in grace.[2] The provincial synods and local presbyteries were ordered to dismiss Remonstrants who might be serving churches under their care. In the years to come, the official Reformed Church adhered rigidly to the doctrine defined at the 1618—19 Synod of Dordrecht, and its major theologians interpreted these statements by elaborating their meaning according to Aristotelian categories.

 The controversy between the Arminians and the orthodox Calvinists had political consequences. The two leading Dutch politicians of the period took different sides in the dispute. Maurice of Nassau (1567—1625; stadtholder of the Dutch Republic 1587—1625) backed the Gomarists and Jan van Oldenbarneveldt favored the Remonstrants. Politics as well as religion separated these men. Maurice wished to make his family (the House of Orange) monarchs; John wanted the merchant aristocracy to control the country. Doubts have been cast on Maurice's religious sincerity, since he once said that he did not know whether predestination was blue or green, but his strong orthodox stand allied him with the staunchly Calvinistic masses of the towns. At the time of the Synod of Dordrecht, Maurice moved against his enemies. Oldenbarneveldt was arrested, tried, and beheaded; Episcopius was exiled; and others, such as Grotius, were imprisoned. The Arminians seemed to be finished in the Netherlands. But by 1625, when Maurice died, they were allowed to return, and the Remonstrant church that they founded has continued to our time. Frederick Henry (1584—1647), who succeeded his brother Maurice, realized that a rigid orthodoxy was as unsuited to the Netherlands as was an absolute monarchy. The various faiths in the area could not be forced to conform without grave danger of economic ruin. In the long run the result of the bitter struggle over Calvinism in the Netherlands was an official policy of toleration.

Though the Arminian quarrel in the Netherlands was settled, albeit by force, the debate has reappeared periodically. England provided the most fertile soil for the growth of Arminianism. Many Laudians (followers of William Laud 1573—1645, a High Churchman who became archbishop of Canterbury 1633) accepted the more liberal view and passed the teaching on to the latitudinarians (i.e., those tolerant of variations in doctrine). During the 18th century the Unitarians were Arminians, as was the great evangelist John Wesley. Through Wesley's Methodism, Arminianism has come down to our time as an important theology. The Arminian-Reformed arguments are still a matter of great concern.

LUTHERAN VERSUS REFORMED

Just as the Reformed were confronted with the problem of Arminianism, so the Lutherans had to deal with a number of controversies during the later Reformation era. As in the earlier stages of the Reformation, theological and political problems were intertwined. The Peace of Augsburg (1555), which settled the first period of the religious war within the Holy Roman Empire, gave too little political and legal security to the German Protestants. It was concluded with the understanding that a final settlement of the problems would be made at a later time. But when the theologians representing the Lutherans and the Roman Catholics met at Worms in 1557, the divisions among the Protestants encouraged the Catholics to postpone a settlement. The arguments among the Reformed were complicated by the spread of Calvinism in Germany. Rulers, such as Frederick III (1515—76; elector of the Palatinate 1559—76), introduced Calvinism into their principalities. Though he departed from the Lutheran position, Frederick claimed to follow the Augsburg Confession (in the form of the *Variata*[3]), so that he could be protected by the rights guaranteed to those who confessed this symbol. Other German Reformed theologians and princes followed his example.

Among the other divisions of German Protestants were the Gnesio-Lutherans ("True Lutherans"), a group that followed Matthias Flacius Illyricus (1520—75) in rejecting the ideas of Melanchthon and his followers (called Philippists after Melanchthon's given name). Flacius, a Slav, was a skilled humanist before he came to Wittenberg; he accepted Luther's doctrine of justification by faith. Later he taught at Wittenberg and Magdeburg and then settled at the University of Jena. He made the latter school a center for conservative Lutheran doctrine. Brilliant and controversial, he wrote a church history called *Magdeburg Centuries,* which remains of great interest. Flacius and the Gnesio-Lutherans attacked Melanchthon for being too conciliatory toward Roman Catholics and proceeded to develop Lutheran teaching not only in distinction from Catholicism but also in opposition to the doctrines of the Philippists. In the Adiaphoristic Controversy of the mid-16th century the Flacians attacked their opponents for making concessions to Catholicism in the matter of church ceremonies. The "True Lutherans" stated that nothing is an adiaphoron (a matter of indifference) if it touches on any aspect of Christian truth. Many other conflicts followed, but perhaps the most important involved the attempt to clarify the Lutheran doctrine of the Lord's Supper.

The Lutheran teaching of Holy Communion, while rejecting the Catholic dogma of transubstantiation, held firmly to the Real Presence of the body and blood of Christ in, with, and under the bread and wine. An important early Protestant, Huldreich Zwingli (1484—1531), leader of the Swiss Reformation, held that the Lord's Supper is only a memorial or sign of a spiritual partaking of Christ. John Calvin tried to harmonize Lutheran and Zwinglian views by stating that the body and blood of Christ are truly received, but in a spiritual manner by the believer along with the elements of communion.

In the controversy that began in 1552 between Joachim Westphal (1510—74; a Lutheran) and Calvin over Eucharistic views, the differences between the Reformed and the Lutheran position were sharpened. Melanchthon and his followers, who refused to become involved in the debate, were accused of being in sympathy with the Calvinist position and were denounced as Crypto-Calvinists. So the debates within Lutheranism were embittered by the presence of Reformed teaching in Germany. Lutherans and Calvinists agreed on many matters, but the Reformed tended to reject liturgical worship, stressed a greater participation in the solution of social problems, and differed in doctrine concerning Christology and the sacraments.

Another group of Lutheran theologians included Jacob Andreae (1528—90) and others who tried to establish a mediating position. With centers in the Universities of Leipzig, Rostock, Marburg, and Tuebingen, they tried to preserve Lutheranism by avoiding extremes. Their efforts led to the adoption of the Formula of Concord, a confessional statement aimed at settling the controversies by replacing the separate creeds of the various Protestant territories. At the root of the arguments that plagued the Lutherans was the interpretation of the Augsburg Confession. The Formula of Concord took notice of many different interpretations and provided a definitive statement for future theologians. The Formula was published with the three ecumenical creeds (Apostles', Nicene, and Athanasian), the Augsburg Confession and its Apology (i.e., Defense), Luther's two catechisms (small and large), and the Schmalkaldic Articles in the *Book of Concord* (1580). This work became binding on two thirds of German Protestantism, making for a clear doctrinal difference between Lutheran and Catholic teaching as well as between Lutheran and Reformed teaching.

Systematization of doctrine could now take place within Lutheranism. As a result, Lutheran doctrine came to be expressed in elaborate statements based on proof texts. This method, used in simple form by earlier Lutheran leaders, flowered in the work of Johann Gerhard (1582—1637). His *Loci communes theologici* is an outstanding statement of Lutheran orthodoxy.

The Reformed theologians and princes of Germany had tried but failed at Frankfurt in 1577 to unite on the basis of a kind of Reformed formula of concord. The Heidelberg Catechism of 1563 continued as the main doctrinal statement of German Calvinism. The University of Heidelberg was the intellectual center of the movement that came to include such territories and cities as Nassau, Bremen, Anhalt, Hesse-Kassel, Cleves, Julich, and Berg. An important milestone in the spread of the Reformed faith in Germany was the conversion of Elector John Sigismund of Brandenburg (1572—1619; elector 1608—19) from Lutheranism to Calvinism in 1613. John, who had studied at Heidelburg, defended his new position in a statement entitled *Confessio Sigismundi* (1614). Partly as a result of this shift, Brandenburg's alliances with Saxony and the Hapsburgs ended, and a new one was established with the Palatinate.

The Protestant rulers of Germany were henceforth divided into two groups: Lutherans (led by the elector of Saxony, who tried to keep the old order intact) and Reformed (led by the elector Palatine of the Rhine, who wished to take an active part in the struggles of the Calvinists of western Europe). Hatred between these two groups kept the Protestant forces divided and enabled the Counter Reformation to make impressive gains.

ROMAN CATHOLIC VERSUS PROTESTANT

In the mid-16th century Roman Catholicism seemed to be a dying faith. In Germany, for example, by 1555 nine tenths of the people and nearly all of the secular princes had become Protestants. The rulers of many other parts of Europe, it appeared, might become the heads of newly established national churches similar to the Church of England under Henry VIII (1491—1547; king 1509—47). But, as a result of the Counter Reformation, this did not happen.

The Roman Catholic Church reacted to the Protestant

challenge in various ways. Catholic doctrine was defined more precisely at the Council of Trent (1545—63), and various decrees were passed demanding moral reform. The teachings of Trent were spread by establishing new schools, often with the aid of religious orders. Printing was controlled by enforcing the Index of Prohibited Books and by various licensing laws in the Catholic states of Europe. The Inquisition and other types of courts and other institutions fostered repression of Protestant ideas. For example, Carlo Borromeo (1538—84; cardinal and archbishop 1560), responsible, as archbishop of Milan, for the church in Switzerland, sent representatives there to determine why the reformers had been highly successful there. According to the reports they brought back, ignorance and immorality of Swiss priests had enabled the Protestants to defeat them in arguments before the city councils. This resulted in establishment of Reformed churches in cities where debates had taken place. Borromeo then established the Helvetian College in Milan to train priests for Switzerland. By 1600 there was a well-educated Catholic clergy in the country and the Protestant advance was halted. Later, colleges were built in Switzerland to assure a trained ministry for the Swiss Catholic Church.

New religious orders, such as the Jesuits, were also useful in countering Protestantism. In Poland their work met with outstanding success. Calvinists had won the majority of the Polish nobility and at the Diet of Warsaw (1573) had secured religious freedom as a constitutional right. Working closely with the kings of Poland, who remained loyal to the Catholic cause, Jesuits brought many members of their order into the land and established several colleges. Sigismund III (1566—1632; king of Poland 1587—1632, of Sweden 1592—1604, crowned 1594; called "king of the Jesuits") insisted that his followers be Catholic to enjoy royal favors. Under royal pressure many nobles renounced their Protestant faith, returned to the church, and evicted Protestant peasants from their lands. Officials and judges, educated and influenced by Jesuits, aided the Catholic Church to recover church buildings and property. By the 17th century most of the educational institutions of Poland had fallen into the hands of Jesuits, insuring that those who reached positions of authority would continue to uphold Catholicism. In 1607—08 Protestant lords were involved in a revolt among the nobles against Sigismund. With the suppression of this insurrection the power of the Protestants was broken, and Catholicism triumphed in Poland.

Of all the areas of Europe torn by the conflict between a reformed and revitalized Catholicism and Protestantism, the most tragic is the Holy Roman Empire. Within the empire, Bavaria and Austria became the center for the reestablishment of Catholicism in Germany. One of the problems of history is to explain why Protestantism lost its drive after 1565, whereas Roman Catholicism became increasingly more confident. Perhaps it was because of disappointment over social conditions. Though the Reformation had reestablished sound doctrine, it had not made the impact on society that many of its 16th-century proponents had predicted. Superstition, immorality, and social injustice continued to flourish in Reformed countries. Protestants as well as Catholics found human beings very resistant to change.

As the Roman Catholic Church regained power in Germany, a strain was placed on the terms of the Peace of Augsburg (1555), which had settled the 16th-century religious wars. According to the treaty, rulers in each area had to choose between Roman Catholicism and Lutheranism, and their subjects had to conform to the official religion or leave the territory. Another provision of the Augsburg peace provided for an "ecclesiastical reservation," that is, if a Catholic spiritual ruler of an ecclesiastical territory became Protestant he was to give up his lands. This was an attempt to halt the secularization of church property. It also secured for a Catholic the three ecclesiastical votes for the Holy Roman Emperor.[4] But there was no adequate legal provision to enforce the ecclesiastical reservation. As a result, when a dispute occurred its outcome depended on the strength of the contending parties.

An example of the problems that arose was the incident involving the conversion of Gebhard Truchsess (1547—1601;

elected archbishop of Cologne 1577) to the Protestant faith. In 1582 he announced his intention to become a Protestant, marry, and make both Catholicism and Lutheranism legal in his domain. The ecclesiastical reservation was invoked, and an army established the Catholic Duke Ernest of Bavaria (1554—1612; archbishop of Cologne 1583—1612) in Gebhard's place. Truchsess was promised Protestant support, but only a small army from the Palatinate came to his aid, because Lutherans suspected that he favored Calvinism.

An Imperial Diet at Regensburg (Ratisbon) in 1608 tried but failed to remove Protestant-Catholic tensions. In 1608 the Evangelical Union was formed. It consisted of most of the German Reformed and Lutheran princes. Heavily influenced by Calvinists and under leadership of Frederick IV (1574—1610; elector of the Palatinate 1592—1610), the union included Ansbach, Baden, Neuburg in the Palatinate, and Wuerttemberg; Brandenburg, Hesse-Cassel, Nuernburg, Strasbourg, and Ulm joined in 1610; Saxony did not join. In 1609 the rival Catholic League was formed under leadership of Maximilian I (1573—1651; duke of Bavaria 1597—1651). War preparations began, but individuals of good will on both sides tried to reach a settlement without armed conflict. Resolving issues between Protestants and Catholics became ever more difficult, as the dispute over the succession to the rule of Julich, Berg, Cleves, Mark, and Regensburg indicates. After five years of negotiation the conflict was resolved by assigning Cleves, Mark, and Regensburg to Protestants and Julich and Berg to Catholics.

THE THIRTY YEARS' WAR

Though each side felt that war was inevitable, the outbreak of the Thirty Years' War surprised both. Before tracing the course of the conflict, it is helpful to have some general characteristics of the war in mind.

By the time the fighting was over, most European states, including France, Spain, Sweden, Denmark, Bohemia, and the various principalities of Germany, were involved. The war can be divided into four main phrases: Bohemian (1618—25), Danish (1625—29), Swedish (1630—35), and French (1635—48). The length of the hostilities and the hundreds of thousands of soldiers involved in the conflict devastated the areas where the fighting took place. The turmoil began as a religious conflict, but during the final phases it was primarily a political contest. The Catholic Bourbon house of France, frightened by the growth of Hapsburg power, sent troops and money to support the Protestant cause. The political, dynastic side of the struggle led to the Peace of Westphalia, which ended the war. The settlement is, in a sense, the first modern international peace treaty, a precursor of the Congress of Vienna (1814—15) and the Treaty of Versailles (1919).

The Thirty Years' War began in Bohemia. The king of this Slavic land, which is part of modern Czechoslovakia, was one of the seven electors who chose the Holy Roman Emperor. The king of Bohemia was elected to his position by the nobility, and for nearly a century a Catholic Hapsburg had been chosen. But by the early 17th century many Bohemians were Protestants. Bohemia had been a trouble spot for the Roman Catholic Church since the time of the reformer John Huss (ca. 1369—1415). In the 17th century the most militant Bohemian Protestants were the Calvinists. The Reformed Church and its allies in Bohemia feared the extension of Hapsburg power and the strengthening of the Catholic Church. Their fears seemed confirmed when Ferdinand II (1578—1637), trained anti-Protestant, became king of Bohemia in 1617. Despite promises to the contrary, Ferdinand began to persecute Protestants.

The first open act of Bohemian rebellion was the "defenestration of Prague." On May 23, 1618, two Catholic representatives of the king and their secretary were thrown from a window in the Hradschin Castle but were not seriously injured. Jubilant Catholics hailed the incident as a miracle; Protestants pointed out that the men had landed on a manure pile. After the incident the Bohemian representative assembly, the estates, met to elect a different king. Ferdinand was deposed and Frederick V (1596—1632; elector of the Palatinate 1610—23) became king of Bohemia in 1619. He was a handsome young Calvinist prince, active in the Evangelical Union. Statistically he might have become Holy Roman Emperor, since Protestants now controlled four of the seven votes. But actually Frederick ruled Bohemia for such a brief time that he has gone down in history as "the Winter King." In war with the Hapsburgs he did not receive the aid he expected from the international Calvinist community and the Evangelical Union. Ferdinand, on the other hand, received assistance from Spain, the papacy, Bavaria, and the Catholic League. In November 1620, at the Battle of the White Mountain, west of Prague, the count of Tilly, commanding the forces of the Catholic League, crushed Frederick's troops, and the "Winter King" was forced to flee.

Jesuits soon arrived in Bohemia to force Catholicism on the people. Refusing to knuckle under, 150,000 fled from Bohemia. The old Protestant nobility was eliminated when its lands were seized and given to loyal Catholic Hapsburg supporters. Ferdinand followed up this victory by conquering the Palatinate and forcing Frederick into exile.

The sweeping Catholic victory led other Protestant princes of Germany to support Christian IV (1577—1648; king of Denmark and Norway 1588—1648), who began the second phase of the war. As duke of Holstein the king of Denmark was also a prince of the empire. He had built his power and wealth by controlling the entry to the Baltic Sea, and now he wished to aid the German Protestants while gaining more territory for himself. The Dutch and the English gave him economic aid for a campaign. The Emperor, needing additional support to meet the Danish challenge, struck a bargain with Albrecht von Wallenstein (1583—1634), a strange, sinister, mercenary soldier of boundless ambition. Wallenstein, who had gotten rich from lands seized from Bohemian Protestants, agreed to furnish an army of 20,000 at no cost to the empire. In his campaign against the Danes he showed himself to be an excellent general, forcing Christian to withdraw from the war by 1629.

The Hapsburg Catholic tide was now at its height, and it looked as though forcible conversion would be the order of the day for most German Protestants. Protestant losses were many and great, but none more symbolic or longer lasting than the loss of the Palatine library. Bavarian troops who conquered this area seized the library of Heidelberg, a treasure of manuscripts and books, and shipped it to Rome, where it still is. The Edict of Restitution (1629) decreed the restoration of all lands that Protestants had taken since 1552. It not only upset the Protestant princes, who regarded it as a warrant for their destruction, but Catholic rulers also felt that Ferdinand was using it to increase Hapsburg control over Germany. In addition the princes feared Wallenstein and demanded that his army be dissolved. Ferdinand tried to allay their suspicions by dismissing Wallenstein and disbanding his army.

If the Edict of Restitution had been fully enforced, Protestantism in Germany would have been destroyed. Problems with the German Catholic princes hampered Ferdinand, but the death blow to his dreams came when Gustavus Adolphus (1594—1632; king of Sweden 1611—32) invaded Germany in 1630. A brilliant soldier, statesman, and devout Lutheran, Gustavus was one of the most influential rulers in early modern times. Before his invasion of Germany he defeated the Danes, the Russians, and the Poles. He entered the Thirty Years' War not only to save Protestantism but also to ensure Swedish control of the Baltic Sea. The changing character of the war is indicated by this, that part of the money financing the Swedish expedition came from the Catholic king of France on advice of Cardinal Richelieu. At first the German Protestant princes were frightened by the Swedish armies, but after the sack of Magdeburg they supported them. Gustavus defeated the count of Tilly at the Battle of Leipzig (or Breitenfeld, 6 miles north-northwest of Leipzig) in 1631 and at Rain (near the confluence of the Lech and the Danube) in 1632. These victories enabled him to restore freedom to Protestants in south and southwest Germany. Ferdinand recalled Wallenstein to counter the Swedish menace in the Battle of Luetzen (southwest of Leipzig) in 1632. The Protestants won, but Gustavus was killed in action. The Swedish army remained in Germany, but its influence declined. When Wallenstein decided to assume political power, the emperor dismissed him and had him murdered.

Despite an attempted settlement in 1635, the war was kept alive by the French. Hiring mercenaries at first and later mobilizing a French army, they were determined to reduce Hapsburg power. The war lost nearly all religious significance as it became a dynastic struggle. Superior resources, coupled with the leadership of brilliant generals, caused the tide to turn in France's favor. The Hapsburgs were defeated so decisively that Spain sank to the status of a second-rate power while France took its place as the leading European state.

By 1648 the war was settled in a series of treaties known as the Peace of Westphalia. The settlement was a victory for Protestantism and the German princes and a defeat for Catholicism and the Hapsburgs. Some of the terms of the settlement include the confirmation of the Peace of Augsburg, with the addition of Calvinism to Lutheranism and Catholicism as a religious option for a prince. The treaty allowed Protestants to keep all the lands they had taken from the Roman Catholic Church after 1624. It also recognized the sovereignty of some 350 princedoms, cities, and bishoprics and demanded that the emperor secure their consent before making laws, raising taxes, recruiting soldiers, or making war or peace. Since these petty units argued continually, agreement on most issues was virtually impossible. The independence granted these states made the unification of Germany under a single ruler nearly hopeless. Other significant provisions of the peace included recognition of the Netherlands and Switzerland as independent states, approval of Hapsburg control over Bohemia, restoration of part of the Palatinate to Frederick's heir, the granting of electoral dignity to the Duke of Bavaria (thus making eight electors), and extension of the territories of Brandenburg to compensate for land ceded to Sweden.

The war left Germany so exhausted that recovery took almost a century. Most of the armies had lived off the land. The soldiers, mostly mercenaries, had had no pity on the civilians, had sacked cities and pillaged the countryside, and for amusement had raped, burned, and tortured. Disease and famine helped to reduce the population drastically. A malaise settled on the land, making it easy for France to keep it divided.

The Peace of Westphalia did settle long-standing religious differences. Catholics and Protestants realized that they must live together since neither was strong enough to destroy the other. Forced compromise provided opportunity for toleration. At the time, some did not appreciate this and called for renewed war. Angered by concessions to Protestants, Pope Innocent X (1574—1655; pope 1644—55) declared the anti-Catholic clauses of the treaty invalid. Among the Protestants the exiled Bohemian Brethren demanded that fighting continue until their homeland was restored to them. Neither group gained much of a hearing—a sign that the religious wars in Europe had ended.

THE ENGLISH REVOLUTION AND THE CAUSE OF TOLERATION

One of the few major European countries not directly involved in the Thirty Years' War was England. Internal troubles so occupied the attention of the English that continental involvement was not possible. The 17th century began with the death of Elizabeth I and the accession to the throne of a new family, the Stuarts, in the person of James I (1566—1625; James VI of Scotland 1567—1625; James I of Great Britain 1603—25). He was highly educated, intellectual, and the author of several works, including *The True Laws of free Monarchies*. But he was naive about English affairs. The Tudor dynasty before him had been despotic, but they cultivated popularity with the people. James tried to follow in their footsteps, but his authoritarianism upset the English. The major problem facing him was the struggle with Parliament, which, though it was not a democratic institution, was a powerful group, representing (in the House of Commons) rich town merchants and the leading country families. The conflict that James began was to last through four Stuart reigns and transform England into a constitutional monarchy, with the House of Commons, rather than the king, as the real ruler of the land. Underlying the struggle were different philosophies of government. The theory of the divine right of kings was that God had placed the sovereign on the throne as His representative, and that anyone who resisted the king was acting against God. Parliament, on the other hand, supported the historic rights of Englishmen and held that control over one's person and property is not to be taken away without the consent of the individual involved (secured either directly or indirectly). The courts of common law helped Parliament protect the rights of the common man and check the king's power.

The Stuarts and Parliament clashed over religion, economics, and rights.

(1) The literature of the period is marked by frequent mention of *religion* as the cause for the struggle. The House of Commons was taken over by the Puritan party, a group within the Church of England that demanded simpler church services and a more pronounced Protestant theology. Anticipating a Protestant attitude on the part of the Scottish Calvinist king, the Puritans, in April 1603, gave James the Millenary Petition (named from the Latin for "a thousand"; its authors claimed 1,000 signatures for it). It asked him to stop offensive customs, such as making the sign of the cross in baptism, wearing certain vestments, and using a ring for marriage. The petition also asked that clerical marriage be allowed and that ecclesiastical abuses be eliminated. In 1604 James met with the Puritans at Hampton Court. His sole concession was that a new translation of the Bible be undertaken. The King James Version appeared in 1611 and has had a profound effect on English and American culture. Puritans fought a running battle with James in Parliament. They wanted him to intervene on the Protestant side in the Thirty Years' War and they wanted Charles, his son, to marry a Protestant princess. They failed in both.

James argued with the Protestants but did not favor Roman Catholics. The Jesuits encouraged attempts to assassinate him. The most famous attempt was the Gunpowder Plot of 1605, in which conspirators led by Guy Fawkes (1570—1606) tried to blow up the king and Parliament. Many Catholics were executed. An oath of allegiance was required of those who were not taken into custody. The English were haunted also by specters of the "Black Legend," a term associated by Protestants especially with the anti-Protestantism of Philip II (1527—98; king of Spain 1556—98).

The reign of Charles I (1600—49; king 1625—49) saw the religious strife intensify. James was a Calvinist. Charles was an Arminian. The latter's reign was marked by a division in the church as a result of growing Arminianism among the clergy. In 1633 Charles appointed William Laud (1573—1645) archbishop of Canterbury, with instructions to enforce a universal liturgy even if it meant driving the Puritans from the church. In some respects, such as doctrinal matters, Laud was more tolerant than the Puritans, but he sought complete outward uniformity of worship. It was a matter of supreme importance to him that the Communion table be placed at the east end of every church and that all should bow when the name of Jesus was mentioned. Using the Court of High Commission and the Court of Star Chamber (where royal power prevailed), he vigorously enforced severe sentences on nonconformists. Over 20,000 Puritans emigrated to New England while Laud was in power.

(2) *Economics* also divided the monarchy and Parliament. The House of Commons was part of the revenue-collecting system of the English kings. Lacking patience to work with Parliament, both James and Charles tried to raise money on their own through forced loans, ship money, forest fines, knighthood, and the granting of monopolies. The people hated these taxes, many of which were based on old laws that had not been enforced for years.

(3) The issue of *rights* took several forms. One problem involved free speech in Parliament; another, resistance to forced loans; and yet another, arbitrary imprisonment. In order to secure revenues, Charles I in 1628 signed the Petition of Right, which safeguarded Englishmen from arbitrary taxes and illegal

imprisonment as well as other royal abuses. But Charles dismissed Parliament and for 11 years ignored this document.

By 1640 Charles was at war with the Scots and desperate for money to secure an army. He therefore summoned an assembly, called the Long Parliament (1640—53; dated by some to 1660), which became a rallying point for opposition to royal absolutism. Puritan forces in Parliament joined the Scots (1643), and England was plunged into a civil war. A little known member of Parliament, Oliver Cromwell (1599—1658), showed himself to be a military genius in leading the rebel forces (called "Roundheads" because they wore their hair cut short) to victory over the royalists (the "Cavaliers"). The king was captured and executed in 1649. The nation then came under the control of Cromwell, who became Lord Protector in 1653. A church settlement to replace the Anglican establishment was attempted by the Westminster Assembly (1643—48/49; met irregularly thereafter until 1652/53), but the Presbyterianism agreed upon by the clerical representatives in attendance was not enforced. Fragmentation of the Puritan position led Cromwell to be more tolerant. National life during the Commonwealth (1649—60) was heavily influenced by Calvinist Puritanism. The Christmas festival was abolished, the marriage ceremony was made a civil act, and plays were forbidden.

When Cromwell died, a desire for stability led Parliament to invite the son of Charles I to return as king. Charles II (1630—85; king 1660—85) had spent many years in exile in France, where he had come to admire the absolutism and Catholicism of Louis XIV (1638—1715; king 1643—1715). Neither of these qualities were to endear him to the English people. He kept the "Cavalier Parliament," elected in 1661 and overwhelmingly royalist, in session until 1679. It passed a series of acts called the Clarendon Code, which provided legal basis for persecution of Puritans. Over 2,000 clergymen lost their pulpits, and over 5,000 persons were jailed as a result of these laws. Other provisions excluded Puritans from posts in city governments. In 1670, in the secret Treaty of Dover, Charles promised Louis XIV to restore Catholicism to England as soon as possible, in return for French subsidy. But when he tried to do this, in 1673, by allowing freedom of worship in private homes, Parliament reacted so violently that he abandoned the plan and remained Anglican until his deathbed confession of Roman Catholicism.

James II (1633—1701; king of England, Scotland, and Ireland 1685—88), successor of Charles II, tried more openly to restore Catholicism. He appointed Papists to command the army and to teach at universities. To win support among the dissenters (Puritans), he included them in his first Declaration of Liberty of Conscience (1687; he issued a second in 1688). But when seven Anglican bishops were charged with treason for not supporting the Declaration, they were found not guilty. Anglicans (Tories) and Whigs (Puritans) united against the king and offered the throne of England to William (1650—1702; Prince of Orange, France; stadtholder of Holland 1672—1702; king of England 1689— 1702) and Mary (daughter of James II; 1662—94; married William 1677; queen of England, Scotland, and Ireland 1689—94) in 1689. James fled to France, and William and Mary took the throne without opposition. This came to be called the Glorious Revolution. Later in 1689 Parliament passed the Toleration Act and the Bill of Rights, which guaranteed civil rights and parliamentary supremacy and extended freedom of worship to all except Unitarians, Roman Catholics, and Jews. A provision in the Toleration Act stated that only Anglicans could serve in the government and the army, but even this restriction could be lifted by the dispensing acts. Even limited toleration was a great step forward in the history of human freedom.

The new English parliamentary government found justification in the political writings of John Locke (1632—1704). His *Two Treatises of Government* argue that government is a contract between a ruler and the citizens and that revolution is justified if the contract is broken by arbitrarily denying the people their natural rights to life, liberty, and property. He also claimed that the most effective form of government is based on a representative system. In one of the ironies of history, Locke's apology for the revolution of 1688 was later used by American colonists in 1776 in revolt against the British.

2.

Theology and Culture
in the Age of Orthodoxy

SCHOLASTIC THEOLOGY

A long period of controversy followed the rediscovery of the Gospel by the 16th-century Protestant reformers. The quarrels that resulted from the breakup of the medieval church led to definition of the Protestant position. The philosophy of Aristotle was used by participants in debates to express their ideas. The Christological issue among the Lutherans, the predestinarian disputes among the Reformed, and the debate between the two over the Lord's Supper encouraged precise definition of doctrine. The Neo-Aristotelianism of the theologians was part of a general trend in post-Reformation Europe to return to Aristotle. Popular in such southern European schools as Padua, Italy, and Coimbra, Portugal, Aristotelianism spread to the Protestant universities of Germany by the late 16th century. Early in the 17th century a movement developed called Protestant Orthodoxy. Among the outstanding Lutheran leaders of this Age of Orthodoxy were Johann Gerhard (1582—1637), Johann Konrad Dannhauer (1603—66), Abraham Calov (1612—86), and Johann Andreas Quenstedt (1617—88). Their Reformed counterparts included Johannes Wolleb (1586—1629), Johann Heinrich Alsted (1588—1638), Gisbert Voet (1588—1676), and Francois Turrettini (1623—87).

Lutheran orthodoxy was not dead orthodoxy. It lived and flourished, as witness its useful productions. Johann

Gerhard, outstanding Lutheran dogmatician, studied philosophy and medicine at Wittenberg. In 1605 he became lecturer at Jena, superintendent at Heldburg 1606, general superintendent at Coburg 1615, and professor of theology at Jena 1616. His most famous work was *Loci theologici*. He also wrote polemical books, Bible commentaries, homiletical aids, and works on the Christian life.

Johann Konrad Dannhauer studied at Marburg, Altdorf, and Jena and was professor and pastor at Strasbourg. Famous for his preaching and teaching, Dannhauer found time to write over 50 works covering the entire scope of theology and including a series of polemical treatises against Roman Catholics, Calvinists, and Syncretists.

Abraham Calov, born in East Prussia, was educated at Koenigsberg and Rostock. He became pastor and teacher at Koenigsberg in 1637 and at Danzig in 1643 and professor at Wittenberg in 1650. Despite a busy life, he wrote more than most people read in a lifetime. His dozens of volumes, many numbering thousands of pages, cover the major topics of 17th-century theology and include 28 works dealing with the syncretistic controversy. Perhaps his major achievements are *Biblia illustrata* (a commentary on the Bible), and *Systema locorum theologicorum* (a 12-volume systematic theology).

Johann Andreas Quenstedt was a professor at Wittenberg. A man of quiet, kindly, irenic disposition, he wrote *Theologia didactico-polemica*, one of the greatest Lutheran theologies.

> Although this enormous volume would have cost a pastor many weeks' salary, it went through five editions between 1685 and 1715. One might say that Quenstedt's *System* killed systematic theology in the period of Lutheran orthodoxy as Michelangelo killed Renaissance art by the unexcelled quality of his work. Quenstedt's lifework is so big, so complete, so concise and systematic, and so excellent that no later Lutheran ever came close to equalling it.[1]

Prominent among Reformed scholars was Johannes

Wolleb. He was born and educated in Basel, Switzerland, where he became a pastor and professor of Old Testament studies. His most famous of many works was the *Compendium theologiae Christianae*. Because of its sound theology and clear arrangement, it was used as a text in many Reformed universities.

Johann Heinrich Alsted, born at Ballersbach, near Herborn, Germany, was educated at Herborn. Remaining at his alma mater as professor, he wrote dozens of volumes that made him famous wherever the Reformed faith had secured a foothold in Europe. He attended the 1618—19 Synod of Dordrecht and supported its condemnation of Arminianism. The Thirty Years' War forced him to move to Transylvania, where he became professor in a new school that the Calvinist prince of that land had established. He remained there until his death. Alsted not only applied Aristotelian logic to theology in such works as *Theologia scholastica didactica* but also tried to unify all knowledge in *Encyclopaedia scientiarum omnium*. His approach was typical of many Protestant scholars who tried to put into a single work the whole range of knowledge—metaphysics, logic, geology, and the other sciences. Using a variant of scholasticism developed by Peter Ramus, Alsted wrote the *Encyclopedia septem tomis distincta*. These volumes were widely used throughout the academic world of the 17th century. Cotton Mather (1663—1728) said that one could "make a short Work of all the Sciences," for it was a veritable "North-West Passage" to them.[2]

Gisbert Voet, a Dutch Calvinist, was educated at Leiden and later became a minister. His pastoral activity, which began in 1611, took him to places where Roman Catholicism and Arminianism were popular, thus providing him with opportunity to develop a polemical style. An industrious person, he taught Arabic, Syriac, logic, physics, metaphysics, and theology and preached eight times a week. His major work was completed at Utrecht, where he became professor of theology and Semitic languages in 1634. While serving in that post, he attacked Descartes, Cocceius, the Arminians, and any others who differed with him. One factor that led to such polemicism was his insistence on a life of devotion and strict morality. Voet's outlook is very similar to that of the Pietists, and his severe moralism led him to sympathize with the English Puritans. His major works include *Disputationes selectae theologicae; Desperata causa Papatus;* and *Exercitia et bibliotheca studiosi theologiae.*

Francois Turrettini was educated at Geneva, Leiden, Utrecht, Saumur, Montauban, and Nimes. He was pastor (from 1648) and professor (from 1653) at Geneva, where he fashioned a theology opposed to many 17th-century trends. Basing his study on Calvin's writings and the Canons of Dort, he wrote *Institutio theologiae elencticae.* Though discredited in the 18th century, it profoundly influenced American Presbyterians through the Princeton theology of Charles Hodge (1797—1878) and others.

The goal of Protestant Orthodoxy was to unify all theology and harmonize the remainder of knowledge with an understanding of God. It produced massive works, tightly outlined through many divisions and subdivisions, and diffi-cult for the 20th-century mind to appreciate. The Age of Orthodoxy was to continue until the 18th century, when rationalism and Pietism superseded it. Orthodox theologians tried to present their views in standard form, i.e., as the doctrine of salvation and of the means for attaining salvation. Orthodox teaching relied on Aristotle and certain medieval logicians for the nature of its arguments, but its basis was Scripture.

Orthodox Lutheran dogmatic expositions fol-lowed the order of the history of salvation: Creation, the Fall, Redemption, and the Last Things are the major points which always appear in such presen-tations. The doctrine of the Word and the doctrine of God are set forth first. The usual order in the various "loci" typically included the following: (1) the Holy Scriptures, (2) the Trinity (the doctrine of God, of Christ, of the Holy Spirit), (3) Creation, (4) Providence, (5) Predestination, (6) the Image of God, (7) the Fall of Man, (8) Sin, (9) Free Will, (10) the Law, (11) the Gospel, (12) Repentance, (13) Faith (justification), (14)

Good Works, (15) the Sacraments, (16) the Church, (17)
the Three Estates, and (18) the Last Things.[3]

The central tenet of 17th-century Orthodoxy emphasized the Bible as the fundamental presupposition of theology. Scripture was trusted as God's Word, and the external statement was not differentiated from the underlying meaning. Orthodoxy believed that God inspired the prophets and apostles to write the message they received from Him. The divine Word they communicated was preserved in Scripture without error; therefore the Bible is the infallible norm for Christians as well as the court of final appeal in all theological arguments. Orthodox theology taught that the Scripture is its own best interpreter and that difficult passages are to be interpreted with the aid of clear ones. Great emphasis was placed on the literal interpretation of Holy Writ, taking it in its ordinary and apparent sense.

As the discussion moved on to the doctrine of God, Lutherans were especially concerned with the way the divine and the human natures of Christ are united in one person. They debated how the natures effect one another, or how the divine and human attributes interact in Christ. As to creation, they held that God first made an unformed mass and completed creation in six days. Man was considered the crown of God's work but fell through sin. Because of the unity of the race the corruption of sin passed from generation to generation. According to this explanation, without regeneration humans are under the wrath of God and subject to both temporal and eternal punishment.

As Lutherans and Reformed defined the subject of evil and sin, they parted company. The Calvinist idea that God preordained and carried out evil according to His secret will (the basis for the teaching of double predestination) was rejected by the Lutherans, who held that God permits evil and that He sets limits to its exercise but is not responsible for it. Lutherans found comfort in the doctrine of single predestination (to salvation). The elect, they taught, are those whom God predestined to salvation; the reprobate are those of whom

God foresees, but does not predestine, that they will not have saving faith at death.

Lutherans maintained that one can pass from spiritual death to life only through the operation of the Law and the Gospel. The Law is God's eternal and unchanging wisdom for righteous living. Summarized in the Ten Commandments, it demands acts of goodness as well as a pure heart. But man is unable to obey the Law so its role is not to save but to condemn. Forgiveness comes only through Christ's redeeming love and sacrifice as proclaimed in the Gospel and is received in penitent faith. Evangelical teaching in the Age of Orthodoxy differed from that of medieval Christianity on the doctrine of repentance. Rather than stating with the medieval church that repentance (or penance) consists of contrition, confession, and absolution, it held that repentance involves only contrition and faith. Contrition is the proper effect of the Law, which threatens, accuses, and condemns; faith is the proper effect of the Gospel, which comforts, edifies, and saves. By giving people an insight into sin and into the punishment of God, the Law drives a person to repentance. The Gospel brings forgiveness through Christ and comforts the believer. It was clear that works play no role in repentance. Good works, excluded from merit of salvation, were considered the fruits of faith. The deeds that the Christian performs were regarded as a means of glorifying God and helping one's neighbor.

Orthodoxy taught that the sacraments (Baptism and the Lord's Supper) were the New Testament counterparts of circumcision and the Passover. Old Testament sacrifices were regarded as types of the coming Messiah. Baptism and the Lord's Supper applied God's promise of forgiveness to the individual. The invisible church was believed to be the congregation of all saints and believers. The visible church includes all who profess faith in the Gospel. Those who associated with Christ in only an external way will be separated from true believers on the Day of Judgment. When that time comes, the world will be destroyed by fire, believers receiving eternal life and the wicked being cast into hell.

This summary applies to the major writers of the age, but as the 17th century unfolded, many details were elaborated and subtle shades of difference developed. It is important also to remember that there were several points of tension between Calvinists and Lutherans.

THE CLERGY

Doctrines were explained to the laity by pastors who were largely controlled by secular rulers. One of the unforeseen consequences of the Reformation was a reduction in the status and number of clergy in Protestant lands. In contrast to Roman Catholics and Anglicans there were few aristocrats among the German Protestant clergy. Ministers were usually chosen from the lower classes and were looked down upon by the nobles. In the universities the theological faculty was the only one open to the poor. Protestant clergymen produced under such circumstances had less polish and capacity for adjusting to higher society than their Roman Catholic counterparts. But what they lacked in sophistication and understanding of the world they made up in book learning that sometimes bordered on pedantry. By the end of the 17th century the typical parson had studied at a university and worked as a teacher or tutor before beginning his ministry. Village pastors had to supplement their income by such activities as farming, beekeeping, or brewing. At times local nobles would hire pastors as grooms or tutors. City ministers were higher than the village pastors on the social scale, but the most favored members of the clergy were the court preachers and theological professors. Lutherans were especially respectful of the theological faculties, and out of this tradition grew the 19th-century belief in academic freedom for the universities of Germany.

Congregations served by these clergymen were passive. They had no rights, no organization, and little control over the pastor. Territorial rulers issued edicts for the church much as they would make laws for secular affairs. Every aspect of church life was controlled by the princes. They saw to it that the church had no bishop, synods, or other aspects of independent rule. Through his appointed consistory the ruler controlled church finances, arranged discipline, and chose the clergy. Usually the churches were under the direction of a general superintendent, and each diocese had a director to see that the regulations of the prince were observed. Visitations settled disputes, and reports were given to the ruler.

Princes controlled not only the legal structure of the church but also doctrinal areas. Often the ruler had little theological knowledge, and his intervention was hasty, thoughtless, and inconsistent. Territorial rulers became "Protestant Popes" for their subjects. Various theoretical justifications were advanced that allowed a ruler to keep his power while giving the church a measure of freedom. Johann Gerhard reasoned that the church was divided into three groups: the clergy, the civil authority, and the rank and file of the laity. Each estate had its particular task in life. For example, the civil rulers were responsible for the government; the clergy were to punish, advise, and administer the sacraments; the people were to follow the directions of the ruler and clergy. The power in such a system was the civil ruler who directed the other two groups. The prince was the divinely appointed guardian of the spiritual as well as of the material welfare of his subjects.

To further strengthen the ruler's position, arguments were often advanced that were based on treaties with Roman Catholic powers (for example, the Peace of Augsburg, 1555). These elaborate justifications stated that the rights formerly exercised by the hierarchy of the Roman Catholic Church had devolved on the civil rulers of the German Protestant states. Therefore whatever the pope was able to do in former times, the princes could now do. Other writers went beyond the devolution argument, teaching that the pope and his representatives had usurped the original divine right of the prince. They held that civil rulers received their power directly from God and acted on His behalf.

But in either case, whether their authority came through the claims of the Roman Catholic Church or directly from God, the princes had absolute power in their own territories. Yet it was clear to the theologians that rulers were not bishops. The magistrates were not to preach and administer the sacraments but to see that these duties were properly performed by appointed ministers. The pastors for their part were to support the prince and encourage a submissive attitude on the part of their parishioners. Princes were believed to be accountable to God alone for their sins. No clergyman would dare to exercise church discipline against a secular ruler, since that would be regarded as a sign of disobedience.

The effect of princely control and scholastic theology on the preaching of the period was often unfortunate. The detailed scholarship so characteristic of the era carried over into the pulpit. Johann Benedikt Carpzov the elder (1607—57) said that there were 100 different modes of preaching. Another said that there were 26. Johann Gerhard advocated 11 styles of preaching: (1) grammatical, (2) logical, (3) rhetorical, (4) histrionic, (5) ecclesiastical, (6) historic, (7) esthetical, (8) scholastic, (9) elenctic, (10) mystical, and (11) heroic.

Another characteristic of sermons of the period was scholarly verbiage, which made them hard for the average person to grasp. Gerhard, who was a pastor while he was a professor, used Latin, Greek, and Hebrew in sermons because he felt that this lent added emphasis.

The Orthodox clergy included also much sensational and imaginary material in their sermons. In an attempt to add interest to scholarly detail, the preachers used fables, stories, illustrations, strained metaphors, and strange images. Titles of sermons or sermon collections that indicate this include "Heaven's Kiss of Love," "Bitter Oranges and Sour Lemons," "Pale Fear and Green Hope in Sleepless Nights," "Splendid Poverty," "Salted Sugar," "Heaven in Hell," and "The Only-Begotten Twin." Carpzov delivered a yearlong series of sermons in which he compared the Lord to various workmen, including a welldigger, a lantern maker, and a cloakmaker. Another preacher drew a parallel between the devil and a vicious dog and showed how Satan bit Adam and then bit Christ in the leg and how Christ drove him back to his kennel in hell. On another occasion the same preacher delivered a sermon comparing Christ to a chimney sweep and discussed the sweeper, the flue, and the broom.

Despite the style of scholarship, strained expression, and polemical approach, the clergy of the period could boast of many deeply spiritual colleagues who were conscientious in the care of souls. Gisbert Voet advised Christians how to lead a godly life. He prescribed prayer, fasts, vigils, and solitary devotion in the soul's war against the world, the flesh and the devil. He included a chapter on "euthanasia, or the art of dying," and another on visitation of those who need consolation. Johann Heinrich Alsted wrote a detailed work on casuistry, in which cases of conscience are arranged in accordance with the articles of the Creed and the Ten Commandments. Calvinists showed a greater interest than Lutherans in church discipline. Lutherans practiced private confession on the basis of the Catechism and its form of absolution.

As the Age of Orthodoxy settled over the Protestant area of Europe, the Roman Catholic Church enjoyed renewal in France. After the Edict of Nantes (1598) had given Protestants legal and civil rights, the Huguenots (French Calvinistic Protestants) lost much of their zeal. A great revival of Catholicism paralleled the Protestant decline. The healthy state of the Roman Catholic Church and clergy in France coincided with other areas of national achievement. The 17th-century saw the golden age of French literature, with such writers as Pierre Corneille (1606—84), Moliere (1622—73), Jean Baptiste Racine (1639—99), Jean de La Fontaine (1621—95), and Francois de La Rochefoucauld (1613—80). These geniuses encouraged the clergy to artistry in preaching and religious writing. The political and social atmosphere of the land also stimulated the ministers. Louis XIV delighted in hearing a minister preach who not only was eloquent but also passionately believed what he said. The clergy, encouraged by the king's attitude, hoped to make him a better person and through him reach the entire nation. The king's interest in religion made church attendance fashionable at court and aided the church in its influence on French life.

The freedom given to the Huguenots also encouraged the Catholic clergy of France to greater faithfulness. For much of the century the Roman Catholic Church could no longer depend on persecution to counter Protestantism but was forced to use preaching and a faithful, caring ministry to win people. A remarkable group of clergy rose to meet the Huguenot challenge, including Francois de Sales (1567—1622), Vincent de Paul (1580/81—1660), and Jacques Benigne Bossuet (1627—1704).

Francois de Sales was a Savoyard who was educated at Paris and Padua. Ordained in 1593, he did missionary work in a part of Savoy (an area in southeastern France and northwestern Italy) that was under the spiritual influence of the Genevan Calvinists. Achieving remarkable success in his ministry, he became bishop of Geneva in 1602. His loving, patient attitude coupled with his outstanding preaching made him a favorite with Henry IV of France. Not only was he an effective preacher, but he also did much religious writing. His popularity has been the inspiration for the founding of several religious orders.

Vincent de Paul was born in southwestern France and educated at Dax and Toulouse. He was ordained in 1600. In 1625 he founded the Lazarist Order, and in 1634 he helped found the Daughters (or Sisters) of Charity. Deeply spiritual and influenced by Francois de Sales, Vincent stressed the Incarnation and man's total dependence on the merits of Christ.

Bossuet, born at Dijon, France, was educated at Paris and soon achieved fame for remarkable preaching. He was brilliant, with a remarkable knowledge of the Bible, the church fathers, and the intellectual trends of the century. As bishop of Meaux he was drawn up into the major religious conflicts of the day, which involved Protestant conversionism, Quietism, Jansenism, Gallicanism, and Biblical criticism. He also found time to tutor the dauphin, serve as court preacher, and gain election to the French academy. Throughout a long and busy life he managed to write several books and is still remembered for his vigorous defense of the divine right of kings.

WITCHCRAFT AND THE BEGINNING OF SCIENCE

The Age of Orthodoxy saw the rise of modern science. Some writers refer to the era as the period of the scientific revolution and hold that it prepared Europe for global leadership in the 19th century. The first phase of this important intellectual change began about 1560. It was a time when old ideas were challenged by a new outlook. The second period began during the mid-17th century and featured the work of Isaac Newton (1642 Old Style—1727). He replaced the theocentric outlook with a centerless secular one that has been the basis of the Western intellectual outlook ever since.

The idea that most 16th-century Christians accepted about the world had been inherited from the ancient Greeks. Elaborated by medieval scholars, this view taught that every being, according to its degree of perfection, had a place assigned in the universe. This great chain descended from God and the angels through the physically perfect stars, planets, sun, and moon to the four elements of the world (earth, air, fire, and water). The universe was believed to be geocentric, with the earth at the center, surrounded by circling planets and the fixed stars. Although at variance with 20th-century cosmology, this view fits the observed phenomena. Christian theology seemed to receive support from the geocentric theory. Man was in the center of God's creation, where Christ had come to perform His saving ministry. The hierarchical structure of the universe assured man that God was in control. The sun's movement around the earth seemed to be verified by Joshua's command that the sun stand still (Joshua 10:12-13), by Eccl. 1:5, and by several statements in the Psalms.

Historians have suggested that people at the time of the scientific revolution began to question the geocentric cosmology because they had more accurate measuring devices, or had developed better mathematics, or made a series of "fortunate guesses." Whatever the reason, early scientists did break down prevailing assumptions about the universe but could not immediately arrive at a new consensus. The most famous scientific pioneer was Nicolaus Copernicus (1473—1543). He assigned the central place in the universe to the sun and held that the rising and setting of the stars could be explained by the earth rotating on its axis. It has been thought that he developed the heliocentric theory to simplify his calculations. Despite his modifications Copernicus retained much of the medieval system. Johannes Kepler (1571—1630) advocated more sweeping changes, which condemned the medieval view to oblivion. Kepler explained that the planets move in an elliptical rather than a circular fashion about the sun. Galileo Galilei (1564—1642), through the use of a telescope, provided many observations that tended to confirm the heliocentric theory.

The new science eventually destroyed the Aristotelian synthesis and caused those who wished to defend the older view to become more narrow and belligerent. In this connection, possibly as an offshoot of a combination of factors, belief in witches increased. In such an atmosphere heretics and socially different people were regarded as servants of the devil. The period from about 1600 to about 1680 saw the high point of witchcraft in Europe. By the 1690s the only major action against witches occurred in New England. During the years when witch trials were common, it was believed that thousands of women and some men made secret agreements with the devil and regularly attended sabbats. Travel to the sabbat assemblies was said to be supernatural, involving the use of flying broomsticks or winged goats. Those who attended these meetings worshiped the devil, who appeared either as a black-bearded man, a toad, or a goat. After listening to strange music and participating in revolting acts of homage, the witches engaged in sexual orgies with Satan and his servants. Often feasts of roast children, fricassee of bat, or exhumed corpses were held. When not attending these assemblies, the witches were expected to suckle familiar spirits in the form of bats, toads, or moles and to cause infertility in newlyweds, disease, and storms.

Evidence for the existence and behavior of witches was secured by torture. Though horrible torture might make a person confess anything, it seems that many in the 17th century believed they were witches. Most of those who confessed to witchcraft were cruelly executed.

Scholars in the Age of Orthodoxy included discussion of witchcraft in their works and even published encyclopedias on the subject. These works insisted that every detail of witchcraft was true and that all objections to the persecution of these emissaries of Satan must be stopped. Most writers on the subject believed that the number of witches was increasing and that the reason for such a sorry state was the leniency of judges. Undoubtedly the struggle in Europe between Catholics and Protestants led to the renewed emphasis on witchcraft. Protestants were just as insistent as Catholics on the reality of witches.

But with the spread of belief in Newton's explanation of the world, interest in witchcraft declined. Newton provided a new synthesis after earlier scientists had destroyed the medieval world view. As a professor at Cambridge University he managed to construct a model of the universe and a way of reasoning that became acceptable to most people. His work is based on the universal law of gravity, which postulated that every particle attracts every other particle with a force that is proportional to the product of their masses and inversely proportional to the square of the distance between their centers. To arrive at this solution, he devised a new mathematical technique, the infinitesimal calculus.

Newton published his findings in a massive Latin work entitled *Philosophiae naturalis principia mathematica*. The *Principia,* as the book is commonly known, demonstrated the law of gravity in relation to the planets and included the science of mechanics, defining force, momentum, and inertia with mathematical precision. After proposing the law of gravity, Newton showed that the pull of the moon and that of the sun caused tides, that the earth and the other planets are flattened at their poles, and that the path of the comets can be traced because they are under the sun's influence.

Newton established the methodology of much of modern science. Included in it are three principles: (1) Insistence on experimental observation. He was very suspicious of general ideas and felt that whenever possible they should be tested by experiments. (2) The law of simplicity. When there are several valid explanations for a phenomenon, the simplest one is to be accepted. (3) Extensive use of mathematics, expressing the universal law of gravity as a formula. The combination of experimental observation and mathematics has proven very successful for science.

Newton could use mathematics to a greater extent than his predecessors because of the progress made during the 17th century. In the year 1600 Roman numerals were still commonly used. Modern symbols for multiplication, division, and addition were not accepted. Much mathematical work was done in a literary form. A virtual explosion of mathematical knowledge changed all this by the year 1700. In rapid succession decimals, logarithms, analytical geometry, laws of probability, and calculus were developed. Practically every philosopher or thinker had to be a mathematician.

Between 1630 and 1700 most educated Europeans came to accept the heliocentric viewpoint and the mathematical-mechanical description of the universe as Newton explained it. The emphasis on uniform law and rationality led to the decline of belief in witchcraft. Evil beings in league with the devil could not easily exist in a world run by Newtonian laws. A sample of the new way of thinking was the reaction of the judge at one of the last witchcraft trials in England. He dismissed the case with the sarcastic remark that there was no law against traveling between London and Oxford on a broomstick.

HYMNS AND DEVOTIONAL LITERATURE

The warm and vibrant faith of the Age of Orthodoxy is not always clearly evident to us in the theological works of the period. But the hymns and devotional literature of that time are different. Suffering and turmoil produced great poets and poignant expressions of the Christian faith. In many ways this was the golden age of Lutheran hymnody, with such great writers as Philipp Nicolai, Johann Heermann, Johann von Rist, and Paul Gerhardt.

Nicolai (1556—1608) was a pastor and theologian in Westphalia. He lived through the dreadful experience of the plague. Though he buried 1,300 people within six months, he wrote the words and music of "Wake, Awake for Night Is Flying." Note the first verse of this hymn so rich with Scripture and the assurance of God's care:

> "Wake, awake, for night is flying,"
> The watchmen on the heights are crying;
> "Awake, Jerusalem, at last!"
> Midnight hears the welcome voices
> And at the thrilling cry rejoices:
> "Come forth, ye virgins, night is past!
> The Bridegroom comes, awake,
> Your lamps with gladness take;
> Alleluia!
> And for His marriage feast prepare,
> For ye must go to meet Him there."

Nicolai also wrote "How Brightly Beams the Morning Star." These two works are called, respectively, the King and the Queen of Chorales.

Johann Heermann (1585—1647) was a pastor at Koeben at the time of the Thirty Years' War. During his ministry the city was almost destroyed by fire; it was sacked four times by Wallenstein's armies and in 1631 was visited by the plague. Heermann was forced to flee for his life several times. He also lost all his possessions. Yet it was during this period in 1630 that he wrote the beautiful hymn, "O Dearest Jesus, What Law Hast Thou Broken." The following verse expresses his faith:

> Whate'er of earthly good this life may grant me
> I'll risk for Thee; no shame, no cross shall daunt me;
> I shall not fear what man can do to harm me,
> Nor death alarm me.

Other well-known hymns by Heermann include: "Jesus, Grant that Balm and Healing"; "O God, Thou Faithful God"; and "O Christ, Our True and Only Light."

Johann von Rist (1607—67), a prolific writer, was made poet laureate in 1644 by Ferdinand III (1608—57; king of Hungary 1625—57; Holy Roman emperor 1637—57). He suffered greatly in the Thirty Years' War when his home was plundered and his possessions seized. Yet he wrote 680 hymns, most of which speak comfort to those in trouble. His hymns include "Break Forth, O Beauteous Heavenly Light"; "Arise, Sons of the Kingdom"; and "O Living Bread from Heaven."

The leading hymnist of the period was Paul Gerhardt (1607—76). Born in Saxony, he served as a tutor for many years after his graduation. In 1657 he was appointed to a church in Berlin, where he became famous as a preacher. Urged by the ruler of Prussia, he became involved in discussions concerning union between Calvinists and Lutherans, but he refused to compromise the Lutheran position. His intransigence in this matter cost him his pulpit, and he was removed in 1666. For awhile he had no parish and was in a desperate situation, but in 1668 he became archdeacon at Luebben, where he remained until his death. His wife and four of his five children preceded him in death.

In the furnace of affliction Gerhardt wrote 134 German and 14 Latin hymns—hymns that have a subjective mood based on his own experiences and that mirror personal misfortunes and the social calamities of his age. Gerhardt conquered his doubts through faith in God, based on the Lord's workings in nature, the church, and Scripture. Deeply conscious of sin, he realized the forgiving power of the grace of God. Some of his better-known hymns include "O Sacred Head, Now Wounded"; "Evening and Morning"; "Jesus, Thy Boundless Love to Me"; and "O Lord, How Shall I Meet Thee."

In the Calvinistic areas of Europe there was not much hymn writing until the influence of Pietism was felt. For many years the Reformed totally rejected "hymns of human composure" and polyphonic composition. Instead they used material versions of the 150 psalms set to tunes. The psalms were sung in unison and without the accompaniment of "popish instruments."

The deeply religious feelings of the Age of Orthodoxy can also be seen in devotional works. Such literature consists of edifying and popular presentation of the Christian faith for use by individuals and groups gathered informally for prayer and meditation. Many of these books were similar to such late medieval mystical works as *Imitation of Christ,* by Thomas a Kempis. The Lutherans developed specialized prayer books for different occupations, for soldiers and travelers, and even for expectant mothers. They also had meditations and prayers designed to be read at certain times of the day. The most famous 17th-century devotional works were by Johann Arndt (or Arnd; 1555—1621); *Books on True Christianity* and *Little Garden of Paradise.* Arndt was educated at Helmstedt, Wittenberg, Strasbourg, and Basel before he became a pastor and church administrator. His books emphasized mysticism in the interpretation of the Christian life by asserting that true belief is not enough to be a true Christian, but moral purification through righteous living is also necessary. Typical of Arndt's writings is the following:

> Because God is pure love, grace, righteousness, goodness, and mercy, man offends Him by his sins. By injustice we offend God's justice, for He is justice itself. By lies we offend God's truth itself. By hate we offend God's love, for God is love itself. God is the highest eternal good, source of all virtue, and highest love.
>
> He forgives us our sins when we sigh and He is always ready to receive us when we turn to Him. He gave us His dear Son and the Holy Spirit, and He gives us Himself. He is our Father and adopts us as children.
>
> A penitent man therefore experiences a very great fear of God's righteousness and judgments which threaten him so seriously inwardly in his conscience and outwardly in plagues.
>
> Therefore man has neither peace nor rest. The whole world sours so that he can neither eat nor drink.

This threat is nothing else than the living sentence of God's righteousness in our consciences.

[Prayer]

I bewail and confess with contrite and broken heart my short-comings and misdeeds. O Lord! My sins are as many as the sands of the sea. But Thy mercy is vast, too, enduring from eternity unto eternity. Therefore be merciful unto me for the sake of Thy dear Son, Jesus Christ. Amen.[4]

Other important devotional books of the period include Lewis Bayly (ca. 1565—1631), *The Practice of Pietie;* Johann Gerhard, *Holy Meditations;* Johann Heermann, *Practice of Piety;* and Heinrich Mueller (1631—75), *Heaven's Kiss of Love.*

BAROQUE ART

At the same time (ca. 1580—1750) a new form of expression, the baroque, replaced Renaissance classicism in many parts of Europe. The word "baroque" is derived from a Portugese word that refers to irregularly shaped pearls. Like some other terms in art history, such as "gothic" and "impressionism," it was first used disparagingly. But many 20th-century critics consider baroque a distinct, complex style with many admirable characteristics. Baroque artists tried to harmonize a number of styles. The result was art characterized by extravagance, decorativeness, and grandeur. A painting of the era featuring a group of figures is clear and natural, but the individuals cannot be visualized by themselves. The suggested movements of the bodies and the direction of the eyes blend together to provide a dramatic situation and create a whole that is greater than the sum of its parts. Similarly, painting, sculpture, and architecture combined to give a unity to the interiors of buildings. The earliest expression of this is found in Il Gesu, a Jesuit church in Rome. Inside the building a painting on the ceiling (*The Worship of the Holy Name of Jesus*) is skillfully merged with the rest of the structure to create a breathtaking effect. The theatrical quality of baroque lent an impressive larger-than-life quality to its productions.

Rome was the center for the new style, which spread throughout Europe. Local areas often tempered the expressions of baroque, but it generally included lavishly ornamented buildings, decorated with cherubs and angels, twisted and bent columns, and intricate designs in gold and marble. These structures included not only churches but also palaces and government buildings. One of the most prominent architects of the era was Giovanni Lorenzo Bernini (1598—1680). He designed the plaza in front of St. Peter's Cathedral in Rome with two great semicircles of colonnades, so that the viewer is overwhelmed with the realization that it is the center of a powerful religious institution.

The baroque style was carried throughout Europe by the Counter Reformation. There was greater emphasis on color and ornamentation in Spain than in other lands. The major Spanish baroque artist was Jose Churriguera (1650—1723). In Salamanca, his native town, he decorated the newly completed cathedral with many bright colors and designed the city square. Spanish baroque influenced Portugal, Mexico, Peru, and Brazil.

Later in the 17th century there was a building boom in the new style in Germany. The rulers of many states there competed in constructing impressive palaces, churches, and monasteries. Some of them tried to complete structures that were far beyond their means. Augustus II (1670—1733; king of Poland 1697—1704, 1709—33; elector of Saxony 1694—1733) commissioned a massive baroque complex in Dresden, but only the first units, including the Zwinger palace, were completed, and even this took 10 years. Many other rulers also left ambitious projects unfinished.

After the defeat of the Turks, who had besieged the city in 1683, Vienna was in a joyful mood. Palaces, monuments, and churches were built in the baroque style, and Gothic buildings were redesigned to match the new construction. The old gothic city was changed and given a unique baroque look. Other places in Bavaria and Austria saw a similar flourishing of baroque.

The new style affected the French, though they tended to incorporate more classicism into their buildings. They also paid more attention to the practical aspects of life and designed more convenient room arrangements. Yet the influence of baroque can be seen at Versailles, the great palace of Louis XIV. Louis disliked Paris as the capital of the French government, so he selected a new site for the royal residence a few miles from the city, near his favorite hunting lodge. Work on the palace began in 1668, and the court moved to Versailles in 1682, though construction was not completed until 1710. Not only was the structure impressive, but it was designed to blend into its surroundings of gardens, statues, fountains, and a grand canal. The entire setting became a pompous, lavish, and impressive symbol of the era of absolutism. In addition to the palaces and parks, French baroque architects built a number of churches, including Invalides and Sainte-Genevieve.

Other art forms also reflected the baroque style. No age has excelled the portrait painting of the 17th century. The greatest master was Rembrandt (1609—69), the Dutch painter who used dark backgrounds and touches of light to study his subjects. Space and light were essential elements in other types of baroque painting as well. Peter Paul Rubens (1577—1640) and others tried to create an illusion of endless space, so that the viewer would think of infinity. In Spain, Diego Velasquez (1599—1660) was the leading painter of the time. He was artist to the royal court, where his main task was to paint portraits of the king and his family. Among sculptors, Bernini was the leader, as he was in architecture. He produced statues for churches, papal tombs, and fountains for the city of Rome.

The musical achievement of the period is widely recognized. It ended the period of polyphonic music and introduced harmonic music. Polyphony, which had dominated in western Europe since the 12th century, was music in which one part was no more important than another. But baroque music consisted of a single element, the melody, supported by harmony. Polyphony was dominated by voice whereas the new style featured instruments. The new music found expression in the opera with its pageantry and exaggerated emotion. It also produced the oratorio, a sacred work for solos, chorus, and orchestra. This was not part of the liturgy and provided an ideal opportunity for new types of music. Oratorios, and the name itself, originated about the middle of the 16th century with musical performances in the oratory of Philip Neri (1515—95) in Rome. The Jesuits used the new music, and the Lutherans also enjoyed it. German Lutherans, who already had chorales, cantatas, and passion music not performed as part of a regular church service, welcomed oratorios.

Two baroque composers, George Frideric Handel (1685—1759) and Johann Sebastian Bach (1685—1750), stand out from their colleagues because of their superb technical ability and musical genius. Handel was a Saxon who settled in England, where his patrons were George I (1660—1727; king of Great Britain and Ireland 1714—27) and George II (1683—1760; king of Great Britain and Ireland 1727—60). He wrote primarily for large public audiences. Even his religious compositions, such as *Messiah* and *Esther,* were intended for public performances in concert halls rather than in churches. He mastered the work of others and made his own style a combination of German, French, and Italian music. Handel's audiences thoroughly enjoyed his music. His themes were drawn from aspects of 18th-century English life, such as folk music, country dances, and even London street cries. He also loved nature, and one can experience in his music tone pictures of the quiet countryside or of storms at sea. He became England's national composer and was buried with honors in Westminster Abbey.

J. S. Bach's life was not very distinguished except for his music. Born into a large, musically inclined family, he fathered 20 children. Bach worked as organist and choir leader in the small towns and petty courts of Germany. If much of his life was routine, his interest in and mastery of music was extraordinary. He tried to hear the leading musicians of his day and copied virtually every piece of music he could find. He wanted to understand how the Italians and the French were composing their works. Bach became an outstanding organist and taught himself to play the violin. Everything that he learned was incorporated into his own compositions.

Bach composed an impressive amount of great music. He wrote church and secular music, chorales and cantatas, suites and concertos, and solos for flute, cello, violin, organ, and harpsichord. His secular music reflected a boisterous humor and a love of life, and many of his pieces were meant as lessons for his students. Bach's true vocation was neither entertaining nor teaching, but service to God. Deeply religious motives encouraged him to labor over the intricacies of such instruments as the harpsichord and to write music. The aim of such stately works as *Mass in B Minor* and the *Passion According to St. Matthew* was to achieve technical excellence coupled with great beauty and thus reflect something of the nature of God. To compose music was for Bach an act of faith, and to perform it was an act of worship.

ABSOLUTIST PRINCES

The forerunners of present day national states were the absolutist monarchies of the 17th and 18th centuries. The model for these states was France, which under the rule of Louis XIV (1638—1715; king 1643—1715) set the pattern for European culture and civilization during much of the Age of Orthodoxy.

Such absolutism is based on the idea that the king is chosen to rule by God and is responsible to God alone for his actions. The ruler was thought to be a divine agent on earth, and consequently it was considered wrong to question his orders. The king's power was to his state as God's will is to the universe. By 1661, with this ideological base for his authority, Louis assumed personal control in France. When he was young, the affairs of state had been conducted by ministers. The royal power was sufficiently established when he took control, so that no group in France was able to challenge his authority.

His emblem was the sun, the center of the universe. He was called the Sun King by his people and the Grand Monarch by others. He expressed his position simply when he stated: "I am the state." All major government affairs were reported to councils that he controlled, and he could imprison people without trial simply through royal order.

Versailles was the magnificent setting for his impressive court. Several thousand nobles lived there, waited on by 4,000 servants. The expense of the court was a great burden on the French treasury. Louis liked ceremony and lavish display, so court life revolved around an elaborate social calendar. The Sun King was the center of activity and the nobles were reduced to the level of minor actors and onlookers.

A day at court began when the king arose and ended when he retired for the night. At these two daily events the leading nobles handed the king his clothes. During the day, life was occupied by serving the king as he went from one activity to another. The nobles spent their time in receptions, gambling, and hunting and at concerts, plays, and balls or engaged in licentious living while they gossiped about others. Flattery and hypocrisy were the keys to success, and the more sensitive people were demoralized and bored. Louis seemed to want it that way. While the nobles were busy with petty court activities, his middle-class civil servants were taking power in the provinces. The nobles were reduced to the status of useless social parasites.

One of the few individuals whom the king trusted with power was his finance minister, Jean Baptiste Colbert (1619—83). A brilliant, hard-working administrator, Colbert was devoted to his king and country. He directed commerce, industry, agriculture, the colonies, art patronage, and finance. He introduced order into financial administration and eliminated much graft. Under his capable leadership state revenues tripled, but the many wars in which Louis engaged made it impossible to maintain a balanced budget. Colbert believed that the economic as well as the political affairs of the state should serve the king. The policy that he devised to accomplish this, mercantilism, was destined to be very popular in 18th-century Europe. It called for the careful regulation of economics by government, and it contrasts sharply with the later teaching of free enterprise capitalism. Colbert believed that a hoard of gold and silver was necessary for a strong nation. Because France did not have precious metal mines, it would have to export more than it imported in order to increase gold and silver stocks. With this in mind, he encouraged industries that engaged in international trade, and he built a larger merchant marine. Colbert stressed the need for colonies as sources of raw materials and as markets for finished goods. He undertook expansion of domestic trade through improved communications, including the building of better roads and canals, and the abolition of internal tariffs. French business was encouraged to be as self-sufficient as possible. Colbert served his king well, but his efforts to solve French financial problems failed. Added to the cost of incessant warfare, the excessive paternalism of his system tended to stifle initiative and cause more economic problems.

Louis and Colbert were successful in their efforts to encourage literature, science, and the arts in France. Academies were founded that brought expression in the French language to a peak of perfection. Indeed, French replaced Latin as the general language of Europe. Other aspects of Louis' policy were less fortunate. In spite of lessons learned from the religious wars, Louis would not tolerate religious dissent. The Huguenots suffered most from his policy of religious conformity. In 1679 he began a series of actions designed to force them to become Catholics, though their religious rights had been guaranteed. Most Protestant churches were destroyed, schools were restricted, and troops were quartered in Protestant homes (with orders to be as offensive as possible). A campaign was simultaneously launched to convert Huguenots by offering them tax exemptions and bonuses. In 1685 the Edict of Nantes, the legal basis for Protestant rights, was revoked. Over 200,000 Huguenots fled the country, taking their considerable skills to the Netherlands, Prussia, England, and America.

Louis sought further fame by his military adventures. He wished to enlarge France to what he considered its natural boundaries: the Rhine and the Alps. The vast expenses of these wars tarnished whatever glory he might have achieved. The wars fought by Louis included the War of Devolution (1667—68), the War of the League of Augsburg (or of the Grand Alliance, 1689—97, over the Palatinate); and the War of the Spanish Succession (1701—14, over uniting the crowns of France and Spain). These conflicts made France feared throughout Europe, but they weakened the land internally. On his deathbed Louis advised his great-grandson and heir to avoid further wars.

The absolutist methods of Louis XIV became popular througout Europe. Nowhere was the combination of bureaucratic centralization, a standing army, and subjugation of the nobility applied with more success than in Prussia by the Hohenzollern dynasty. The parts of northeast Germany that were the base of their power, Brandenburg and East Prussia, did not seem very promising in the mid-17th century. Much of the area was a poor sandy place devastated by the Thirty Years' War. The remainder of their holdings consisted of small isolated areas that stretched to the Dutch border. Yet Prussia became the determining force in German history and during the 19th century was the nucleus around which Germany was unified. The three leaders who were responsible for the rise of Prussia were Frederick William ("the Great Elector"; 1620—88; elector of Brandenburg 1640—88), Frederick William I (1688—1740; king 1713—40), and Frederick II (the Great, 1712—86; king 1740—86).

The elector Frederick William began to rule during the troubled times of the Thirty Years' War. He managed to increase his possessions at the Peace of Westphalia. To build a strong state, he relied on two institutions, the army and the bureaucracy. By the end of his reign, the Prussian army was recognized as one of the finest in Europe.

The Prussian bureaucracy became one of the most efficient and most highly centralized in the world. The nobles

(Junkers) were forced out of governmental power, and their places were taken by the middle-class civil servants. The elector invited emigrants to settle in Prussia. The Huguenots were among those who came. When the Edict of Nantes was revoked, thousands of them settled in Prussia, and their skills served to enrich the land. The elector followed mercantilist policies, such as high tariffs, trade restrictions, and subsidies to encourage industries. Roads and canals were built and an efficient postal service was established. Frederick William entered the Polish-Swedish War and secured clear ownership of East Prussia. As Duke of Prussia, he became one of the crowned heads of Europe, rather than just another petty German prince.

After the death of the Great Elector, his coarse, hard-working grandson Frederick William I continued his work. The new king was a strange person. He was miserly, had a violent temper, and hated lazy people. A deeply pious Protestant, he considered theaters to be temples of Satan and closed them. Despite his peculiarities, King Frederick William built an impressive army. He spent four to five times as much on the army as on all the other state activities. Under his direction Prussia, which ranked 12th in population in Europe, had the 4th-largest army. Previously armies had depended on volunteers, mercenaries, or impressment, but a draft system was instituted. All adult males were subject to call, but in practice most conscripts came from the poorest elements of the population. To promote discipline and efficiency, the king introduced savage punishments for even the smallest offenses. Another important innovation was limitation of the officer corps to the landed nobility. Military leaders were given many advantages, including a sound education, a high standard of living, and social prestige.

King Frederick William carried his military emphasis over into the bureaucracy. The king watched over every detail of government. Laziness, corruption, deception, and waste were severely punished. Religion did not escape his control. The church was not regarded as a place where the Gospel of Christ was presented, but as a useful public institution whose main purpose was to teach the populace such valuable attitudes as integrity, loyalty, submission, and obedience. Though Frederick William was a staunch Protestant, he allowed Roman Catholic subjects religious freedom because he did not want them to leave Prussia. He is credited with the founding of Prussian, and later German, despotism and militarism.

Frederick II (the Great) succeeded to the throne of his father, Frederick William I. As a youth Frederick had been unhappy in the spartan atmosphere of the court; he was interested in art, music, and philosophy. His father, determined to break his spirit, burned his son's books, destroyed his flutes, and publicly beat him. At the age of 18 Frederick tried to flee from Prussia, but he was caught and returned home. He was then forced to watch the execution of his best friend and accomplice in the attempted escape. After serving a prison term, he accepted his father's plan for his life. He became a cynical, hard-working absolutist king. His father had built a large army but never used it in battle to any great extent. Frederick risked the Hohenzollern war machine several times to enlarge Prussia. Under his leadership the Hohenzollern dynasty challenged the Austrian Hapsburgs for leadership in central Europe.

Frederick started the War of the Austrian Succession (1740—48), which resulted in Prussian annexation of Silesia. This victory led to The Seven Years' War (1756—63). Worried by the Austrian, French, and Russian alliances, which had Prussia surrounded, Frederick struck first. During the conflict he used considerable skill, moving his armies on interior lines to face first one enemy and then another. Despite his brilliance, he was on the verge of defeat three times. When the war was finally settled, he was thankful that Prussia could keep Silesia. To lose 500,000 men in war seemed to teach Frederick a lesson. During the rest of his reign he worked to keep the peace and to improve Prussia through internal development. Frederick's achievements provided the character and spirit for later German nationalism.

Absolutism was welcomed by the czars of Russia as the land took on many of the characteristics of Western civilization, especially under the rule of Peter the Great (1672—1725; reigned with half brother Ivan 1682—89 and alone 1689—1725). Before his time, Russia was of little importance in European affairs, but after 1700, with the decline of Sweden and Poland, it became an important factor.

During the Middle Ages, the Russians were semi-Asiatic and isolated from Western civilization. The Mongol invasions overwhelmed the early center of Russian culture in the 13th century and established the dominion of the Tartar tribes, to whom Russian princes paid tributes from 1240 to 1480. Russia remained almost untouched by the great developments that brought about modern civilization in the years between 1400 and 1700. It had no large-scale commerce, no middle class, neither Renaissance nor Reformation, and it took no part in the rise of modern science.

Beginning in 1584, Russia experienced a period of disorder that led to the "Time of Troubles," which began about 1598/1604 and ended in 1613. Civil War and foreign struggles with the Poles and Swedes threatened the destruction of the state. In 1613 an assembly restored order by electing Michael Romanov as czar. This dynasty was to rule Russia from 1613 to 1917. Although the early Romanovs sought greater contact with the West, Russia remained primarily an agricultural country without adequate commercial and city life.

The reign of Peter the Great marked a turning point in Russian history. Largely through his efforts Russia became a leading world power. However, he failed to solve the major problems of the land. Peter, more than most absolutist rulers, put the welfare of his subjects last. Personally, the czar was a most unusual person. A giant of a man, he was coarse in manners and speech, had a violent temper, reveled in drunken orgies, and took special delight in torturing others. He did have boundless energy and drive to make Russia a great power. To accomplish his goal, he felt a need for closer contacts with the West. He was the first czar to travel abroad, visiting Prussia, Austria, Holland, and England, so that he could learn firsthand from the more advanced cultures.

Peter's obsession with the West led him to try to change the culture and attitudes of his people. He ordered them to wear Western style clothing and shave their beards. He advocated the use of tobacco, previously considered sinful. Women were brought out of their oriental seclusion. He encouraged education by founding schools, establishing a printing industry, and demanding educated men for the civil services. The most striking example of Peter's Western orientation was the founding of the new capital city of St. Petersburg. Moscow was too conservative and set in its ways to suit him. In 1703 he decided to build a new city in the extreme northwestern corner of the land. He could get no closer to the West and still be in Russia.

After ruthlessly suppressing elements in Russia that opposed his policies, Peter began building the armed forces. He reorganized the administration of his realm using European models. To encourage upper-class men to become army officers, he established the principle that nobility came from state service and not from ancestry. The system that made nobles extremely dependent on the czar remained in effect until 1917. To furnish resources and men for war, he introduced two major reforms: poll tax and conscription. To increase the size of his army, a quota of men was set for each village and town. Conscripts were drafted between the ages of 20 and 25 and were required to serve for life. Troops were supplied with Western materials and trained to fight in European style. Peter also created the Russian navy. By the end of his reign he had over 800 vessels on the Baltic Sea.

Peter also strengthened the nation's economy by negotiating favorable trade agreements with other lands, constructing mills, and encouraging better agricultural practices. Many of his reforms were opposed by the Russian Orthodox Church. As a result, when the Patriarch, the leader of the church, died, Peter did not nominate a successor but in 1702 put himself in control of the office, with only part of the income returning to the church. In 1721 Peter established a Spiritual College, later called the Holy Synod, to govern the church under the direction of the czar. The Orthodox Church in Russia had become a department of state with the priests as low-paid civil servants. Peter also dissolved monasteries, revised the liturgy, and reformed ecclesiastical education.

Many Russians opposed these new practices and joined the Old Believers. These groups had formed before Peter's reign in opposition to change in church ritual. The practices that angered the Old Believers may seem slight to us, but such things as the number of prostrations during the reading of a prayer and the number of fingers needed to make the sign of the cross were very important to them. The reforms that angered them were confirmed at a council in 1666—67. The Old Believers resisted the new ritual, and the increased pace of westernization under Peter further enraged them. Many more people joined them despite intensified persecution. They regarded the official church as apostate and the work of Antichrist. They were treated brutally and exiled or forced to flee to such remote areas as Siberia and Karelia. Their number increased to perhaps 20 percent of the population, and the movement continued into the 20th century.

Peter's reforms were necessary as preparation for a long series of wars. From 1690 to 1724 Russia was continually at war, except for 13 months. The goal of all this fighting was to gain warm water ports on the Baltic and Black Seas. Peter's main enemies were the Swedes and the Turks. In 1700 Russia joined Poland and Denmark in the Great Northern War against Sweden, the power that dominated the Baltic Sea. The allies' expectations of easy victory were frustrated by the military genius of Charles XII (1682—1718; king of Sweden 1697—1718). The Swedes smashed the Russian army, but Peter rebuilt his shattered forces and by 1707 faced Charles again. The Swedes invaded Russia, but this time Peter fell back before their advance and drew them deep into the Russian plains. Like Napoleon and Hitler later, Charles encountered Russia's most effective ally, winter. Weakened by the worst winter in a century, the Swedes were defeated. By the Treaty of Nystad(t) (1721) Russia received much of the eastern coast of the Baltic

Sea. Other campaigns secured territory in south Russia from the Turks and the western coast of the Caspian Sea from Persia. Eighteenth-century Russian rulers, such as Catherine the Great, continued the work of Peter.

3.

The Rise and Character of Pietism

NEW PIETY IN ENGLAND—PURITANS AND QUAKERS

A unique religious movement called Puritanism developed in the Age of Orthodoxy. It was destined to exercise a lasting influence in the English-speaking world. Puritans objected to the worship services and the church government of the Church of England (Anglican Church). The Reformation had come to England through the efforts of such rulers as Henry VIII (1491—1547; king 1509—47), Edward VI (1537—53; king of England and Ireland 1547—53), and Elizabeth I (1533—1603; queen of England and Ireland 1558—1603), and many Englishmen believed that too many Roman Catholic practices had been retained. Puritans therefore wished to purify the church of such corruption. The movement began in the 16th century, but it reached its height in the 17th century, when Puritan ideas were used to justify the revolt against the Stuart kings.

Puritanism grew out of the Calvinist or Reformed tradition, which tended to exclude from worship whatever was not commanded by Scripture. English Calvinists applied this principle with greater strictness than did the Reformed churches of continental Europe. Their program for Christianity in England was to have a godly pastor in every parish who would faithfully proclaim the Word of God, properly administer the sacraments, and discipline immoral church members. God's law, divine grace, and man's response were the main points of religion, according to Puritans. They did not produce an original or subtle theology but rather concentrated on the application of Protestant doctrine to the believer's life. Their emphasis on conversion anticipated the Pietist and the Evangelical movements. Puritan conversion meant a fundamental transformation of one's life and attitudes. The believer was expected to live in a constantly disciplined fashion. Many have condemned or ridiculed the Puritan life-style, but it was a satisfying experience for individuals in the 17th century. As they put it: "Man's chief end is to glorify God, and to enjoy Him forever." Joy was found in worship and a life of duty to God.

The Puritan combined his faith with activities of secular life. Work was not believed to be outside the sphere of Christian concern. During the Middle Ages the term "religious" had been applied to a priest or other full-time church worker, but to the Puritan any vocation, be it that of merchant, lawyer, pastor, or homemaker, was a religious vocation. Dignity was given to all honorable callings.

During the struggle against the Stuart kings in the early 17th century, the Puritan position was adopted by the main group in Parliament. Deeply convinced that God is sovereign over human affairs, the Puritans were not afraid to question the power of the king. The opposition that they mounted led to the defeat and execution of Charles I, but they were not able to agree on the form that the new government should take. The various political and social solutions they offered left Oliver Cromwell (1599—1658) no choice but to establish a military dictatorship.

These disagreements could be detected in the Westminster Assembly (1643—53; met irregularly in its last years). The meeting was called to guide Parliament in its religious decisions. It issued the Westminster Confession, a classic statement of Presbyterianism. One of the major divisions in the assembly involved a split between the Independents (Congregationalists) and the Presbyterians. An Independent, John Owen (1616—83) became Cromwell's adviser on religious matters and championed a pluralistic settlement. Under Cromwell, churches were pastored by Presbyterians, Baptists, or Independents, and

Jews were allowed to settle in England. But freedom of worship was not extended to Roman Catholics and Unitarians.

More radical Puritan sects developed, each seeking to establish its particular vision of the kingdom of God. A group called the Levellers gained many followers in the Parliamentary army. Interpreting liberty in Christ as including political democracy, they advocated universal male suffrage, freedom of religion, and equality before the law. Fearing mutiny, Cromwell suppressed them, but Leveller leaders such as John Lilburne (ca. 1614—57) continued to agitate for their ideals.

The Puritan era saw widespread interest in the prophetic books of the Bible and their application to history. Many Protestant scholars revived the old theory of five monarchies in the Book of Daniel. This theory held that four major world empires, Babylonia (or Assyria), Persia, Greece, and Rome, would rule the world. During the last of these empires the kingdom of God (the fifth monarchy) would come to earth as the millennium, or 1,000-year reign of Christ on earth. Details of the coming age were supplied by careful studies of Revelation, the last book in the Bible. Earlier Protestant Reformers, such as Calvin, had refused to discuss the Book of Revelation and regarded the calculation of the millennium as a waste of time. But by the 17th century, leading mathematicians and scholars discussed the end of the age. Joseph Scaliger (1540—1609) wrote a book on chronology that was used to calculate the time of Christ's final coming. John Napier (1550—1617), the Scotsman who invented logarithms, devoted his genius to apocalyptic speculation. And in the 1640s many believed that the greatest discovery of the time was the interpretation of the number of the beast (666; Rev. 13:18) suggested by a Fellow of Oxford University.

The Puritan Revolution, the overthrow of the Stuart kings, and the ferment that resulted added fuel to the fire of prophetic enthusiasm. The second coming of Christ and the establishment of His millennial kingdom gave meaning to the troubled times through which the land was passing.

One of the more interesting groups that seized upon

these ideas, the Diggers, followed the teachings of Gerrard Winstanley (1609—52), who taught that the earth, because it was God's creation, was common property. They were arrested for planting crops on the common land (something like a public park) at St. George's Hill, Surrey, in 1649. Twentieth-century communists claim that the Diggers were forerunners of Marxism, but in reality they were mystics who hoped to prepare the way for the return of Christ.

The most radical apocalyptic group was called the Fifth Monarchy Men. Basing their beliefs on passages in the Prophecies of Daniel and the Book of Revelation, they taught that there should be no compromise with the old order, but rather a new form of government should be established, composed of saints joining together in assemblies under the control of Jesus Christ.

Baptists taught that the Church of England could not be reformed and that it was necessary for true Christians to separate from the national church and form their own groups. These separatist bodies were to accept members who made a personal confession of faith in Jesus Christ and were baptized as believers. Some have tried to establish a link between the 17th-century Baptists and the Anabaptists, but the connection is tenuous at best. In 1609 a congregation of English refugees in Amsterdam led by John Smyth (perhaps ca. 1570—1612) reorganized themselves along what they considered New Testament lines and were baptized with believer's baptism. In 1611/12 a part of this group under Thomas Helwys (ca. 1550—ca. 1616) returned to England and founded the first Baptist church at Spitalfields, now in London. They were called the General (Arminian) Baptists, and by 1644 they had 47 congregations.

Future growth came largely from another group, the Particular (Calvinistic) Baptists. The first of these churches came into existence in 1638—1640. Their antecedents are in a Separatist or Independent congregation organized in 1616 at Southwark, London, by Henry Jacob (1563—1624). His group held that believer's baptism by immersion was the only valid practice. By 1644 there were seven congregations of Particular Baptists. Though Baptists emphasized the authority and autonomy of each congregation, they cooperated with one another to draft confessions of faith and to deal with common problems, such as raising funds for military needs during the Puritan Revolution. Because Baptists served with distinction in the Parliamentary Army and were staunch Protestants, Cromwell favored them when he was in power. With the restoration of Charles II, they became part of English dissent and as such lost their privileges. By that time there were Baptist churches in America through the cooperation of Roger Williams.

While the mainstream of Puritanism moved in a path that involved a more systematized doctrine and church life, other groups stressed the importance of the mystical experience or inner light. One of the chief mystical inspirations was the work of Jakob Boehme (1575—1624), a German shoemaker. He wrote several mystical books in rather obscure and difficult terminology. He was also very critical of the Protestantism of his day because of its bibliolatry, doctrine of election, and notions of heaven.

One of Boehme's more important English followers was George Fox (1624—91). Reared in a strict Puritan atmosphere, Fox left home at the age of 19 to search for enlightenment. Three years later he came to rely on the "Inner Light of the Living Christ." From that time on he became a traveling minister who did not attend church, condemned religious controversy, and preached that truth is to be found in God's voice speaking directly to the soul. Fox has left a *Journal* of his experiences in which the influence of Boehme can be traced. The followers of Fox were called Friends or Quakers. They took as their central teaching the doctrine of the inner light, that is, that the power of the Holy Spirit is given to all people and is not limited by the Scripture. Since each individual received the inner light, all persons were to be equal in the church. Clergymen were unnecessary, for the spirit would inspire those who should speak.

The movement grew despite persecution. At first it spread mainly among the poorer classes; later, people of wealth and higher social standing joined. In 1681 William Penn, an admiral's son, founded a Quaker colony in Pennsylvania. Quakers remained adamant in rejecting oaths, using Christian names in conversation and wearing simple clothes. Their theology was presented in a more systematic form by Robert Barclay (1648—90) in *Apology for the True Christian Divinity*. Quakers taught the equality of all people, both women and men. They continue to make an important contribution in the 20th century and were among the first to protest horrible prison conditions and slavery. They are known for pacifism, education, charity, honesty in business, and toleration.

After the restoration of Charles II in 1660, Puritans were subjected to intense persecution, and the movement lost its force in England. By that time there were thriving Puritan settlements in New England. The Puritans had come to the new world hoping to establish model communities with properly reformed churches, so that the people of England would be able to see what God would do if His people obeyed Him. Under such leaders as John Winthrop (1588—1649) and John Cotton (1584—1652), the congregational tradition developed. It was established that church members must make a "declaration of their experience of a work of grace." Such a requirement made certain that the church would be in the hands of the elect. In addition, only church members could vote or hold office in the government of the colony.

Puritans were not only interested in a just society, but they were also deeply committed to scholarship. John Bunyan (1628—88) and John Milton (1608—74) were Puritans. Arrested in 1660 during the great persecution, Bunyan spent several years in prison producing such literary masterpieces as *The Holy City* and *Pilgrim's Progress*. The latter work established him as one of the most influential religious writers of all time. In it he traces with vivid imagination, in allegorical fashion, the journey of Christian from the City of Destruction to the Heavenly City. John Milton's two immortal works, *Paradise*

Lost and *Paradise Regained,* deal with the fall and the redemption of mankind. He also wrote *Areopagitica,* a defense of freedom of the press, and *Samson Agonistes,* an allegory based on the life of Samson.

CATHOLIC MYSTICISM AND JANSENISM

Under the leadership of Louis XIV, France became the dominant power in Europe in the 17th century. Its influence was felt not only in politics and economics but also in religion and the arts. The age was a time of renewal for the Roman Catholic Church, encouraged by its rise to a position of undisputed power in France. The improvement in the fortunes of French Catholicism had started before Louis came to the throne. During the last half of the 16th century the land had been ravaged by brutal civil wars between Catholics and Protestants (Huguenots). By the beginning of the 17th century, the conflicts were settled and a period of impressive rebuilding began. Under leadership of such able government ministers as Cardinal Richelieu (1585—1642; cardinal 1622; chief minister of Louis XIII 1624—42), the power of the nobles was cut, and the Huguenots were reduced to submission. It was during the same period that the Roman Catholic Church experienced a revival in France.

As with most periods of ferment and achievement, the age of Catholic renewal produced controversy. There was a struggle over the connection of the French church with Rome as well as arguments involving Jansenism and a new type of mysticism called Quietism. The issue over the liberty of the French church was settled in favor of a firm allegiance to the pope.

Jansenists followed the teaching of Cornelius Jansen (1585—1638), a Flemish bishop. They contended that church ceremonies were obscuring the fact that a person can be saved only through God's love and grace operating on the heart. This love comes to those whom God chooses. Their rejection of free will and their emphasis on predestination were similar to

Calvinism. Indeed, their enemies accused them of being "warmed-over Calvinists." The Jansenists insisted that they were not Protestants, but at the same time they condemned the moral laxity of Catholics and the overemphasis on free will in Catholic doctrine.

Jansenism was brought to France by Jean Du Vergier de Hauranne (1585—1643), abbot of St. Cyran, who won many influential people to his cause, including several members of the famous Arnauld family. A convent at Port Royal became a center of Jansenism. Perhaps the doctrinal teaching of the Jansenists could have been tolerated, but their independent turn of mind and the moral emphasis of their preaching drew them into a series of struggles with the Catholic Church and the French government. Besides encouraging purity and holy living among the clergy and people, they also wished to reduce the secular power of the church. They condemned the Jesuits for "laxist" teaching, i.e., granting absolution on too easy terms. Such laxness, they felt, encouraged immorality. Jansenists themselves led very strict austere lives characterized by simplicity of worship and love for religious culture.

A group of clergymen and pious laymen who believed in Jansenism settled near Port Royal, dedicating themselves to lives of scholarship and contemplation. Among them was Blaise Pascal (1623—62), scientist and philosopher. He wrote *Provincial Letters* to defend the movement, but the work widened into an attack on the whole system of casuistry as practiced by the Jesuits. Pascal claimed that the Jesuits undermined the Christian faith by teaching a morality based on what the average person does, rather than on what he ought to do. Jesuit morality held that the end justifies the means and that mental reservations may be used to qualify one's word. Pascal's brilliant wit and moral fervor struck a decisive blow at the Jesuits. As a sample of Jansenist piety, Pascal does much to commend the group. His early death prevented him from publishing a book designed to win others to Christ. The notes that he kept for the work were collected and published in 1670 with the title *Pensees*. A profound book, it argues in both an intellectual and emotional fashion for the existence of God and the reality of faith. In light of his personal encounter with Jesus Christ, Pascal said: "The heart has its reasons, which reason does not know."

To convince unbelievers of Christianity, he propounded his famous "wager," which combines a skeptical attitude with his own brilliant mathematical works on calculating probabilities as follows: God is a good bet. Men should gamble that God exists and act on the assumption. If they are right, they win all; if they are wrong, they lose nothing.

Louis XIV became involved in the Jansenist controversy. He was alarmed by the large number of influential people attracted to the belief, and he felt that the emphasis on a strict moral life was a condemnation of his own life-style. His Jesuit confessors encouraged him to ask the pope to denounce Jansenism. Clement XI (1649—1721; pope 1700—21) in 1713 condemned the group. The convent at Port Royal was suppressed in 1709 and destroyed in 1711.

By the end of the 17th century, more trouble appeared for the Roman Church in France because of a new mystical group. Quietists, as they were called, were inspired by the teaching of Miguel de Molinos (perhaps about 1628/40—1696), a Spanish priest who resided in Italy and presented his views in *Spiritual Guide*. Molinos proposed guidelines that would eventually lead to union with God. The Jesuits had him condemned and imprisoned. Despite opposition, Quietism spread to France, where its followers emphasized passive prayers as the main Christian activity. The leading French Quietist was Mme. Guyon (1648—1717), a woman from an important family who energetically propagated her views and won many converts. Her teaching, elaborated in *Short and Very Easy Method of Prayer*, emphasized single-minded contemplation of God whereby the soul loses all interest in its own fate. Even the truth of the Gospel paled to insignificance before "the torrent of the forces of God" to which an individual must yield. Bishop Bossuet (1627—1704; bishop of Meaux 1681) warned her to stop such teaching, and others accused her of being mentally unbalanced, but she persisted in presenting her ideas. She was repeatedly arrested and finally condemned by the pope and imprisoned.

The ferment and vigor found in the Roman Catholic Church in the 17th century could match developments in Protestantism. Jansenism parallels Puritanism, and Quietism is in certain respects similar to Pietism.

PIETISM

The Peace of Westphalia, which ended the Thirty Years' War in 1648, allowed each ruler in Germany to choose one of three options as the faith of his subjects: Catholicism, Lutheranism, or Calvinism. Thus was confirmed the independence of a large number of principalities, in each of which the church was dependent on the ruler. The prince was exempted from the discipline of the church and was answerable to God alone. Pastors were treated as employees of the state, and the church was regarded as a useful agency of public policy charged with the duty of teaching such attitudes as integrity, submission, loyalty, and obedience. In this era of stifling state-church religion, Pietism emerged as a renewal of the evangelical fervor of the early Protestant Reformers. The new religious outlook had its roots in mysticism, Puritanism, and Anabaptism.

Pietism may be defined as Bible-centered moralism that results in a personal conviction of sin and repentance. This leads to forgiveness through Christ, personal conversion, a life of holiness, concern for the needs of others, and an emotional experience in worship. Attempts to harmonize faith and reason and an intellectual emphasis were not of much concern to Pietists. For them religion was not reserved for authorities and experts; it was something that had to do with a person's feeling and expressed itself in a pious life of service to others. Pietism insisted that believers manifest Christ in their daily lives. It was a reaction against formalistic creeds and made faith individualistic.

The two early Pietist leaders were Philipp Jacob Spener

(1635—1705) and August Hermann Francke (1663—1727). Spener, called the Father of Pietism, grew up in Alsace and attended the University of Strasbourg. There he studied philosophy, languages, history, and theology. His favorite teacher, Johann Konrad Dannhauer (1603—66), encouraged him to study Luther and helped him understand the evangelical teaching of the grace of God. Dannhauer also suggested that lay people be more involved in the church and that some aspects of theological study be undertaken in the vernacular rather than in Latin. Spener was a serious, ascetic, religiously minded student.

In 1659 Spener left Strasbourg and, according to the custom of the time, visited other universities to broaden his educational experience. In the course of his two-year academic journey he went to Basel, Bern, Geneva, Lyon, Freiburg, and Tuebingen. This tour made a lasting impression on him. While in Geneva he fell under the influence of Jean de Labadie (1610—74), who was then at the height of his career. Labadie was a Reformed preacher who blended Jansenism with Calvinist piety to form a strong experiential, otherworldly, mystical faith that came to emphasize the importance of separation and small group meetings. Spener enjoyed hearing him preach, and several years later he had one of Labadie's tracts published in a German translation.

After returning to Strasbourg, Spener finished his degree, married, and became a teacher and a preacher. His goal was to be a professor, but in 1666 he accepted a call to be senior clergyman in Frankfurt. His duties included preaching at the city's main church, presiding over pastors' meetings, ordaining new ministers and inspecting the parishes. Many of the ministers under his charge were twice his age, but he managed the situation very capably. While in Frankfurt, he tried to secure greater lay involvement in the life of the church, improved catechism classes, urged the authorities to enforce certain blue laws, and began an extensive correspondence with individuals throughout Germany. Later he would be called "the spiritual counselor of all Germany." In 1670, he gathered in his home a group of people who were especially interested in a deeper Christian life. They discussed sermons, prayer life, the Bible, and various devotional books.

Spener was a prolific writer and the work that first gained his reputation and on which his fame rests is *Pia desideria (Pious Desires)*. A Frankfurt printer wanted to publish a new edition of some of Johann Arndt's sermons and asked Spener to write the preface. Spener used the occasion to present his ideas for revival in the church. Later his remarks were issued as a separate book. The work made the following proposals for revival: (1) personal religion should be deepened by greater attention to a study of Scripture; (2) laymen must be more involved in the work of the church; (3) Christians ought to be encouraged to practical works rather than spending all their time in dry theological debates; (4) in all theological disputes a spirit of love must be shown, so that others can be won to Jesus Christ; (5) theological education should be improved with a special emphasis given to the moral and spiritual life of ministers; (6) preaching should be marked with conviction and fervor so that people might be converted. Despite opposition of many church leaders, Spener believed that, if his program were followed, the church would be revived, the Jews converted, and the power of the papacy destroyed.

In 1686 Spener left Frankfurt for a position in Dresden. He hoped to have an influence on John George III (1647—91; elector of Saxony 1680—91). But the elector seldom attended church, and Spener found it necessary to condemn him for drunkenness. The friction between the two men caused Spener's stay to be rather short. During his Dresden years he did meet August Hermann Francke (1663—1727), who was to become his successor as the leader of Pietism

In 1691 Spener left Dresden and went to Berlin, where he served as inspector of churches and as a preacher at the Church of St. Nicholas. He remained there 14 years. He was increasingly drawn into the controversies caused by the spread of Pietism. Something of the bitterness of these debates can be seen in the charge brought by the theological faculty of the

University of Wittenberg that Pietists were guilty of 284 heresies. Spener was called a Rosicrucian, a Chiliast, a Quaker, and a fanatic. His last years were spent not only replying to strange comments, such as these, but also in editing his correspondence and papers for publication. Much of this material provided ethical guidance for his followers in the form of answers to such questions as these: What is to be said about dreams, visions, and special revelation? May a Christian wear expensive jewelry with a good conscience? May he attend a dance or theater? May a Protestant marry a Roman Catholic? Can laymen administer Holy Communion? Can an unconverted pastor proclaim God's Word effectively? Busy with his Master's business until the last, Spener died hoping for a better day for the church.

August Hermann Francke, Spener's chief disciple, was born in Luebeck and studied at Erfurt and Kiel. He taught at Leipzig, was pastor at Erfurt and Glaucha and in 1692 became professor at Halle, where he spent the rest of his life.

Largely as a result of Francke's efforts, Halle became the international center of Pietism. Gifted with limitless energy, boundless enthusiasm, great organizational ability, and a flair for what later ages would call public relations, he created an amazing complex of institutions, including an orphanage, boarding schools, Latin school, publishing house, pharmacy, and Bible institute.

Francke was also the dominant figure on the Halle theological faculty for many years. From this position he inspired many students to serve God as foreign missionaries in such distant areas of the world as America and India. The Lutheran Church in the United States owes much of its growth to these Pietist missionaries. In New England the Puritan minister Cotton Mather (1663—1728) said:

> The world begins to feel a warmth from the fire of God
> which thus flames in the heart of Germany, beginning
> to extend into many regions; the whole world will ere
> long be sensible of it.[1]

Pietism was spread throughout Germany and Scandinavia by graduates of Halle, the publications of such men as Spener, and personal contacts. Many beautiful hymns were written by Pietists to express their faith. A notable area of enthusiasm for Pietism was Wuerttemberg, where Johann Albrecht Bengel (1687—1752) became its leader. Deeply influenced by pietist professors at the University of Tuebingen, Bengel studied the works of Spener and Francke and spent some time in 1713 at Halle. He was an unusual Pietist because of his great dedication to scholarship. From 1713 to 1741 he taught at a seminary in Denkendorf and wrote widely in the field of Biblical exegesis. In 1742 he became a high official at Herbrechtingen and in 1749 at Alpirsbach and influenced many pastors to become Pietists.

One of Bengel's works, *Gnomon Novi Testamenti,* was especially popular. It consists of annotations on each verse and is an excellent example of careful philological scholarship. It was put out in several editions and was translated into many languages. Even today Bible students find it useful. Bengel was also interested in the study of the Book of Revelation. He set 1836 as the year for the beginning of the millennium. Many of his statements in the area of eschatology seem odd. But he was clear and correct in rejecting naive views of progress held by many in the age of rationalism and proclaimed a liberating vision of the kingdom of God.

MORAVIANS AND BRETHREN

Though Pietism began as a reform movement within the established church, several separatist bodies sprang from it. One of these was the Church of the Brethren, another was the Moravian Church. The Brethren began at Schwarzenau, Germany, in 1708, when eight people under leadership of Alexander Mack (1679—1735) were rebaptized by triple immersion. Mack was influenced by radical Pietism and was convinced that the New Testament required separate groups of believers rather than a state church. He had settled in one of the few areas of

Germany where religious dissenters could practice their beliefs. This was the tiny county of Wittgenstein, northeast of Frankfurt, in the hill country between the Eder and the Lahn Rivers. The count who ruled the area risked the policy of toleration because of personal conviction and the need for settlers. By the time the legal machinery of the Holy Roman Empire dealt with them, most of the dissenters had left for the Netherlands. The early Brethren in Wittgenstein restored what they felt were apostolic practices. These included baptism by triple immersion face forward, the love feast (consisting of a meal, the Eucharist, and foot washing), anointing of the sick with oil, laying on of hands for Christian service, congregational church government, and opposition to war, oaths, and worldly clothes.

The Brethren won many converts and churches were established in Switzerland, the Palatinate, and Altona. In most places they were subject to intense persecution.

Their plight in Europe led the Brethren to consider migration to America. William Penn had traveled in Germany, encouraging sectarians to come to his colony. His agents distributed tracts and booklets that made Pennsylvania seem like an attractive place to settle. In 1719 many Brethren left Europe and came to Germantown near Philadelphia. Another group migrated in 1729 under Mack's leadership. By 1735 most Brethren were living in the New World. Those who remained in Europe joined such Anabaptist groups as the Mennonites or died out. The Brethren (or Dunkards, or Dunkers, or Tunkers; from the German for "immerse") became a permanent part of American life.

The Moravians, led by Nikolaus Ludwig von Zinzendorf (1700—60), also developed from radical Pietism. Born into a pietist noble family (he was Spener's godson), Zinzendorf was reared by his maternal grandparents and an unmarried aunt. His grandmother was especially influential in forming his deep piety. She was a gifted person who could read the Bible in the original Hebrew and Greek and participate in the most profound theological discussions. Between the ages of 10 and 16

Zinzendorf attended Francke's preparatory school at Halle. Then he enrolled at the University of Wittenberg for legal study. His relatives insisted on this, though he wanted to be a minister. His social status as a noble would not permit him to become a clergyman. In 1721, after graduation, he took a position as a counselor at the court of the King of Saxony. About that time he received an inheritance, which he used to buy an estate. Frustrated by his inability to become a minister, he felt that he might serve God by directing the religious life of the tenants. A short time later a group of Protestant refugees settled on his property.

These settlers were the remnants of the Old Moravian Hussite Church who were driven from their land by persecution. Under leadership of Zinzendorf they founded a village called Hernnhut (which may be translated either "on watch for the Lord," or "watched over by the Lord"), where they tried to return to apostolic practices. These included the rites of foot washing, the kiss of peace, and the casting of lots. They also worked out the peculiar Moravian practices, such as intense community religious life encouraged by daily services; division of the community into choir groups based on age, marital status, and sex; religious education; and an active program of missions, especially to the oppressed black slaves in the West Indies and to people of preliterate cultures. The emphasis was on a monastic type of life with the unmarried separated by sex and children reared in child-care centers. Every effort was made to encourage a communitarian approach, with common occupations attended by instrumental and vocal music.

The views of Zinzendorf were not entirely reflected at Herrnhut. The Moravians were convinced separatists, whereas he wished to remain a Lutheran. He showed a tolerance toward other creeds and even devised a plan for the reunion of the Protestant, Roman Catholic, and Eastern Orthodox Churches. He was also interested in some rather strange doctrines and mystical practices.

Some accused Zinzendorf of deviation from orthodoxy,

but his views were examined and approved in 1734. Yet in 1736 he was banished from Saxony. Exiled for 11 years, he traveled widely and preached his Pietist ideas wherever he went.

Even before his exile, he had been interested in preaching the Gospel in faraway places and he inspired the Moravians to send missionaries to the West Indies (1732), Greenland (1733), and Georgia (1735). A Moravian mission founded in London was to be a decisive influence in the life of John Wesley.

In 1747 Zinzendorf was allowed to return to Herrnhut, where, with the exception of some time spent working with the church in England, he remained until his death.

METHODISTS

Religious life in England reached a low point in the early 18th century. On every hand there was profanity, inhumanity, and gross political corruption. The lower class was ignorant and depraved. Harsh laws demanded that people be executed for petty crimes. In the midst of such discouraging circumstances the populace turned to drink for solace. Churches were poorly attended, public worship was formal and lifeless, and sermons were vague moral discourses that seldom mentioned the Gospel of Christ.

In this unfavorable environment there were faithful Christians, but their influence was slight. By the middle of the century the revolution in agriculture and industry had begun to transform English life. Farmers were forced from their land and concentrated in new towns around factories and mines. The new settlements had no schools or churches. In this situation the Methodists and Evangelicals, strengthened by Pietist teaching, brought the message of Christ to the poor people in the towns.

Methodism grew under the leadership of the two Wesley brothers, John (1703—91) and Charles (1707/08—1788). Their father was a pastor and their mother, Susannah, was a remarkable woman. She not only bore 19 children (John was the 15th, Charles the 18th), but she also closely supervised their educational and religious development. The Wesley brothers attended Oxford University, where they established a religious club. Their group met for Bible study, frequent observance of Communion, and fasting. Their strict piety caused the other students to call them "the Holy Club," "Bible Moths," and "Methodists." The name Methodist was to be an honorable title for Wesley's movement.

One would have expected that John Wesley would have taught or preached and become an important person in the Anglican Church. Such did not prove to be the case. For a man of his temperament it was not enough to be decent and competent. Christianity had to mean more than that to him. He believed that faith ought to be a vital and living experience, yet he knew that for him it consisted of a formal orthodoxy. His problem was clear: How could he trade his dead faith for a living experience with God? To find the solution he multiplied good works, increased his asceticism, and gave his life to serve as a missionary to the Indians.

John spent the years from 1735 to 1738 as a missionary in Georgia, but his work met with little success. While traveling to America in 1735, he met some Moravians who witnessed to him about their faith in Christ. Their assurance of salvation made a profound impression on Wesley. When he returned to England, he worshiped with them for a time and later visited Herrnhut. At a prayer meeting in London on May 24, 1738 he received assurance of his own salvation as he listened to a reading of Luther's preface to Romans:

> About a quarter before nine, while he was describing the change which God works in the heart through faith in Christ, I felt my heart strangely warmed. I felt I did trust in Christ, Christ alone for salvation; and an assurance was given me that He had taken away my sins, even mine, and saved me from the law of sin and death.[2]

As a result, John Wesley reacted against the moralistic

rationalism of the Anglican church. One of his Oxford friends, George Whitefield (1714— 70), had broken with the Anglican system and was preaching to miners in the fields near Bristol. Wesley struggled with his conscience for a time, but by 1739 he too was preaching in the fields. During the last half of his life, he preached over 40,000 sermons, and journeyed over 250,000 miles, mostly on horseback. He traveled throughout the British Isles as well as to Holland and Germany. At his death there were over 125,000 Methodists and 1,500 Methodist preachers. Good organization, fervent preaching, warm fellowship, personal conversion, and robust hymn singing made Methodists a powerful force in England and America. Some historians have credited the Wesleyan revival with saving England from a violent upheaval similar to the French Revolution.

Preaching in the streets and fields often aroused violent opposition. Wesley meant only good for the poor miners, sailors, and factory workers to whom he preached, yet they frequently tried to assault him. He was the center of dozens of riots, many instigated by a local pastor. Some of his assistants were badly hurt, some even killed. Wesley had an iron will and could stare down a drunken mob. He was small, 5 feet 6 inches tall and weighing 120 pounds, but his absolute fearlessness and complete confidence in God carried him through situations that would have unnerved most others. He even seemed to thrive on adversity. The kind of reaction he received is recorded in his *Journal,* for example in the entry for Sunday, May 30, 1742:

> At seven I walked down to Sandgate, the poorest and most contemptible part of the town, and, standing at the end of the street with John Taylor, began to sing the hundredth Psalm. Three or four people came out to see what was the matter, who soon increased to four or five hundred. I suppose there might be twelve to fifteen hundred before I had done preaching; to whom I applied those solemn words: "He was wounded for our transgressions, He was bruised for our iniquities: the chastisement of our peace was upon Him; and by His stripes we are healed."

Observing the people, when I had done, to stand gaping and staring upon me with the most profound astonishment, I told them, "If you desire to know who I am, my name is John Wesley. At five in the evening, with God's help, I design to preach here again."[3]

This kind of preaching aroused resentment, and he described part of an encounter on October 20, 1743, as follows:

Some said, "No, no! knock his brains out; down with him; kill him at once." Others said, "Nay, but we will hear him first." I began asking, "What evil have I done? Which of you all have I wronged in word or deed?" and continued speaking for above a quarter of an hour, till my voice suddenly failed. Then the floods began to lift up their voice again, many crying out, "Bring him away! Bring him away."[4]

Wesley preached justification by faith, the new birth, and Christian perfection (sanctification). His teaching of perfection, the ethical transformation of the believer, seemed to indicate to his enemies a kind of work-righteousness or self-delusion. Wesley denied both of these allegations, but he did not find it an easy doctrine to explain. He drew his teaching from certain mystical writers, such as William Law (1686—1761), Thomas a Kempis (ca. 1379/80—1471), and Jeremy Taylor (1613—67). Though he insisted that a Christian could be holy in this world, he did not mean that he would be free of all wrongdoing.

There were many intellectual attacks on Wesley's ministry. Some said that the astonishing things that happened when he spoke were evidence that he was driving people mad. Wesley himself stated that he was restoring them to sanity. Others expressed the opinion that the fainting and shouting that often accompanied his services were the result of demonic activity. His tactics also seemed to offend 18th-century standards of good taste. They involved "enthusiasm," which offended most literate people. The better classes of society found any display of emotion repugnant. Wesley responded to these charges with the assurance that he did not encourage fanaticism, religious madness, or claims of direct divine inspiration. He was also criticized for preaching in the wrong places; sermons were to be given only in churches. Many Anglicans felt he was wrong for allowing laymen to preach. He was also accused of being out of order. A clergyman was supposed to obey the bishop, and no bishop had installed Wesley as an evangelist at large. He was breaking the rules of the church. Wesley responded that his ordination to a fellowship at a college was a general charge to preach.

As a loyal Anglican, Wesley had no intention of establishing a new church. His special mission was to preach the Gospel to people unreached by the church and provide for their spiritual nurture and discipline. Following the example of the Moravians, he gathered followers into bands, classes, and societies. The first of these was established at Bristol in 1739. At these meetings members judged each others' spiritual lives and studied to deepen their Christian knowledge. Wesley selected laymen who would be able to help him preach the Gospel to the masses. In 1744 the lay preachers met at a conference (which later became annual) to receive instruction and assignment of their area of work. Wesley was not fond of the idea of lay pastors at first, but he later gave it his warm support. Areas of ministry, called circuits, were established. After one or two years ministers were moved to different circuits. In this form Methodism spread throughout the British Isles. The early history of the movement is characterized by its gradual separation, despite Wesley's reluctance, from the Anglican Church.

Charles Wesley became the sweet singer of Methodism and wrote thousands of hymns, including "Jesus, Lover of My Soul"; "Love Divine, All Loves Excelling"; "Oh, for a Thousand Tongues to Sing"; and "Christ the Lord Is Risen Today."

Within the Church of England, the Wesleyan revival strengthened the Evangelicals. They were Calvinists who stressed conversion, strict morals, simplicity of worship, and a life of service to others. Prominent Evangelicals included John Newton (1725—1807), William Wilberforce (1759—1833), and Hannah More (1745—1833).

John Newton was a seaman who had been captain of a slave ship but was converted and became a minister. He was an outstanding preacher and also wrote such popular hymns as "Amazing Grace"; "How Sweet the Name of Jesus Sounds"; and "Glorious Things of Thee Are Spoken."

William Wilberforce was educated at Cambridge University and later entered politics as a member of Parliament. He was associated with the Clapham Sect (named after a suburb of London), a group of Evangelicals who were active in public life. They persuaded him to lead the fight in Parliament to abolish the slave trade. His efforts were successful in 1807. He also lived to see the complete abolition of slavery in the British Empire in 1833.

Hannah More was a leader in educational activities. She was a patron of the Sunday school movement and wrote many religious tracts for mass distribution.

A more famous early advocate of Sunday school was Robert Raikes (1735—1811), a newspaper publisher greatly concerned for the well-being of children. He organized schools to give religious and moral training to poor young people on the only day on which they did not work. The students were taught to read the Bible and often instructions were given also in arithmetic. The Sunday school was an important step in the development of popular education.

The Methodist revival affected not only the Church of England but stirred also the nonconformist churches, which included such groups as the Baptists, Congregationalists, and Presbyterians, descendants of the Puritans. One nonconformist, John Howard (ca. 1726—90), was involved in improving prison conditions in England. Others joined the Wesleyans in attempts to stop gambling, dueling, cruel sports, child labor, drunkenness, and pornography.

The late 18th century also saw the rise of the modern missionary movement. In 1792 the Baptist Missionary Society was organized through the efforts of William Carey (1761—1834), a self-educated teacher, shoemaker, and pastor. He went to India as a missionary in 1793. Other organizations established for worldwide missions included the London Missionary Society (1795), the Scottish Missionary Society (1796), and the Church Missionary Society (1799). Associations were also formed for distributing Bibles and Christian literature.

The Methodist and Evangelical revival changed the course of history in England. Humanitarian reform, cooperation with industrialization, and the desire to win the lost to Christ gave the English the ability to lead western Europe in its global expansion.

THE GREAT AWAKENING IN AMERICA

During the early modern era the English settled in North America, fought several wars to maintain their control, and finally lost the richest part of the continent to the newly independent colonies in America. By the end of the third generation the 13 English colonies had reached a low ebb in culture and religion. The Church of England, officially established in half of the colonies, had little influence outside of Maryland and Virginia. In Virginia only about 5 percent of the people were church members. New Englanders seemed to have a greater interest in religion, but the conviction that had been the basis of Puritan power had waned. Frontier life seemed to be forcing the colonists into barbarism. For centuries no group of Western European people had been so little exposed to Christian teaching and institutions.

The colonies were rescued from spiritual collapse by the "Great Awakening," a religious movement that lasted in America from ca. 1725 to ca. 1750. It was a mass conversion of people through evangelistic preaching. The movement began in New Jersey among the Dutch Reformed churches with the ministry of Theodorus Jacobus Frelinghuysen (1691—1747). Encouraged by what he saw in the Reformed congregations, a Presbyterian, Gilbert Tennent (1703—64), began evangelistic preaching among the Scots-Irish. Stressing the need for a personal decision for Christ, rather than the mere outward observance of religious ceremonies, his work persuaded many New Jersey Presbyterians.

In 1734—35 the Great Awakening came to Massachusetts through the preaching of Jonathan Edwards the Elder (1703—58), one of the most brilliant individuals America has produced. Edwards was the son of a Congregational minister. After graduating from Yale, he became pastor of the Congregational Church in Northampton, Massachusetts. He had a keen and penetrating mind with a mystical bent and profound religious convictions. Preaching slowly and distinctly with great feeling, he made his listeners aware of the consequences of sin and the horrors of hell. In 1734—35 and again in 1740—43 waves of a religious awakening swept over his community and hundreds professed faith in Jesus Christ. Edwards was surprised at the response to his preaching and could only explain it as the work of God accompanying the proclamation of the Gospel. He did try to analyze and account for the revival in such works as *Some Thoughts Concerning the Present Revival of Religion in New England* and *A Treatise Concerning Religious Affections*. These books assess the beneficial and harmful aspects of the revival. During the next two years Edwards wrestled with a long-established principle of his grandfather, Solomon Stoddard (1643—1729), that moral people, though unconverted, may partake of Communion. After long and earnest controversy over this practice, which he opposed, he was forced from his pastorate in 1749. He moved to an Indian ministry at Stockbridge and later became president of Princeton College.

George Whitefield (1714—70) linked the regional movements of the Spirit into the Great Awakening. Born in Gloucester, he attended Oxford University, where he was closely associated with the Wesleys. In 1735 he was converted and began his preaching ministry. He had a loud, clear voice and could speak with dramatic intensity. His preaching moved thousands, including so worldly a person as Benjamin Franklin (1706—90). He followed the Wesleys to Georgia in 1738. Later he made six other visits to the colonies. His ministry took him from Georgia to Massachusetts, and he preached to

Congregationalists, Anglicans, Presbyterians, Reformed, Methodist, Baptists, Lutherans, and Quakers. Other evangelists followed his example and preached wherever they could get an audience.

Many criticized the awakening. Some condemned the excitement and emotional disturbances of the meetings, offensive features of which included convulsions, laughing, screaming, visions, and trances. Some preachers deliberately encouraged these activities. Many revivalists had harsh words for those who would not join in the meetings.

Support of the revival became a test of faith. This attitude led to divisions in the church. The Presbyterian and the Congregationalists split into the "New Lights" and the "Old Lights." The "New Lights" favored the revivals.

Despite its faults the Great Awakening did much to help the future nation. It led to the founding of churches, increased the seriousness of rank and file church members, and caused a new commitment to missions, which were mainly to American Indians. Prominent among those interested in winning Indians was a prospective son-in-law of Jonathan Edwards, David Brainerd (1718—47), who died before his marriage and whose journals became a popular devotional book. The condition of blacks was also brought to the attention of Christians by the awakening. From 1714 to 1760 the number of black slaves in America increased from 58,850 to 310,000. There were few slaves in the north because they were economically impractical. But in the South, where many workers were needed on the large indigo, rice, and tobacco plantations, slavery developed into a major institution. Blacks as well as whites were converted during the Great Awakening. Most Christian churches did not speak out against slavery, but Quakers and Mennonites did. One of the main advocates of better treatment of blacks was a Quaker, John Woolman (1720—72). He tried to reconcile Indians with whites and worked to improve the status of blacks through the abolition of the slave trade.

The Great Awakening also made a great contribution to education. Among the numerous academies and colleges that were established as a result of the revival, the best known are the University of Pennsylvania, Rutgers, Brown, Princeton, and Dartmouth. Of equal importance was a new mood of understanding that developed between denominations. This more open attitude contributed to the spirit of toleration in the United States, and it provided for an evangelical consensus that still influences the nation.

4.

Pietist Theology and its Influence on Culture

PIETIST THEOLOGY: CHURCH AND SCRIPTURE

The Pietists did not present their views in a systematic fashion, as did the major orthodox theologians of the 17th century. But the main Pietist beliefs can be summarized from the writings of Spener and Francke, who were especially interested in the reform of the church. For reform it was felt that each Christian must have a personal relationship with God. To win others to their ideas they did not elaborate on theological categories but emphasized a life of purity that would demonstrate the power of Christ.

The Pietists' desire to simplify religion led to a spirit of tolerance and religious freedom. Because human beings are finite and limited, and theological knowledge is not precise, latitude must be given to dissenters. Spener felt it best not to insist on uniformity beyond certain basic teachings. His position was summarized in the following statement: "in necessary things, unity; in things not necessary, liberty; in all things, love."

The Pietists agreed with the orthodox that the invisible church consists of all who truly follow Christ, and they regarded the visible church as part of the invisible. They tended, however, to emphasize the invisible more than the visible church. A radical Pietist, Gottfried Arnold (1666—1714), took their teaching to such an extreme that he wrote a book focusing on the invisible (nonorthodox) church. The work, the *Impar-*

tial History of Heresy and the Church, tried to view heretics from their own writings rather than from the charges of their opponents. He claimed to see more truth in some heresy than in the official church theology. So long as the pious remained part of the actual visible church Pietists emphasized the invisible group. When a congregation seemed to live up to their ideals they stressed the visible community, as the Anabaptists had done.

Spener and Francke were orthodox in their view of the sacraments, but their emphasis on the individual's response to salvation tended to change traditional views. They held to infant baptism, but they stressed the possibility of losing the new birth unless one lived in obedience to God. Spener taught that unbaptized children of Christians, Jews, and Turks would not suffer damnation. The Pietists' stress on the subjective side of salvation led many to disregard infant baptism and empha- size a later conversion experience.

Another change that Pietism brought to the view of the church was an interest in apostolic times. The way to revive Christianity, they believed, was to restore the early church. The first step in this direction was to have godly ministers. The pastor was to be the shepherd of the flock and not just another official. To do this he should be well trained, lead a holy life, and preach in a clear and forceful manner. The church also needed a greater involvement on the part of laymen if apostolic power was to return. Pietists reemphasized Luther's teaching of the priesthood of all believers. To encourage lay participation, they tried to break down the distinction between clergy and laity. They also desired a more democratic church polity. In the age of orthodoxy, social class distinctions were extremely important. For example, it was considered a disgrace for an upper class child to be baptized in the same water as a worker's infant. Pietists reacted against such things and at their meetings servants and masters would sit together in equal fellowship. Spener objected to the way the churches were to reinforce the attitudes of secular society. His ideal was a presbyterian form of church government, with congregations hiring their own pastor and both clergy and laymen serving on the governing boards of the church.

The small group meetings that Spener began in Frankfurt also had a place in the restoration of the primitive church. These developed from catechism classes and met on Mondays and Thursdays at Spener's home during the years 1670—82. At these gatherings, sermons, Bible texts, and devotional works were discussed, and prayers were offered. These meetings were not supposed to take the place of regular worship services. Several members withdrew from the church because of them, and Spener became suspicious of the practice. He wanted to remain with the official church and reform it from within, rather than separating from it.

Pietism stressed the authority of the Bible. Spener firmly believed that the Scripture is the verbally inspired word of God. But he parted company with the Orthodox theologians in his insistence that Scripture was supreme over creeds and doctrinal statements. Both Spener and Francke felt that creeds had led people to read the Bible in a narrow way. Too many Christians searched the Scriptures to find texts to prove their theological presuppositions.

Pietists also differed from the Orthodox in emphasizing the practical purpose of Bible study. Scripture was given, they held, for the cultivation of a devotional life rather than as a textbook from which to draw doctrines. The Bible was to be read for encouragement, warning, and consolation. The Holy Spirit was believed to be necessary for a proper understanding of God's Word. Without Him one merely read the cold and dry written word of a book. It was the Spirit that gave life and enlightened the mind of the believer. Spener taught that Christians who pray, meditate, and lead a holy life will understand the deep meaning of the Scripture.

The back-to-the-Bible emphasis of Pietism led to a renewal of expository preaching, i.e., taking a text from Holy Scripture and carefully explaining its meaning. Lay people were urged to study the Bible on their own. Universities were encouraged to offer courses in Biblical theology. Those who were able should master Greek and Hebrew, the languages of the Bible, so they could study it in the original tongues and thus deepen their understanding. Such advice led to a renewed emphasis on philology (word studies), which had characterized the approach of the early Protestant reformers. These studies tended to clash with the philosophical (Aristotelian) emphasis of the Orthodox theologians.

Finally, Pietists emphasized the New Testament. Spener believed, of course, that all Scripture was given by inspiration of God, but he placed the New Testament above the Old. The New Testament as the highest stage of God's revelation to man and the fulfillment of the Old commanded the Pietist's attention.

PIETIST THEOLOGY: SALVATION AND SOCIETY

Pietism taught that salvation must be demonstrated by a holy life. Spener believed that in Luther's day Christians had stressed works and neglected grace. Because of this, the great reformer had preached faith and not works. But Spener felt that his own times were different. Many theologians and preachers in the 17th century taught justification by grace through faith but neglected to present the necessity of good works. At one time in church history there is a need for a certain teaching while another period required a different emphasis. Desiring to link salvation more closely to a godly life, Spener was led to attack the prevailing theology of his day. He felt that the intricate scholastic elaboration of theology, coupled with hostility toward those who differed even on minor points, conflicted with a life of service to others. Doctrine was to be tested not on an academic basis but rather by its effect on the lives of those who held it.

Spener held firmly to the sinfulness of man and salvation through faith in Christ. He stated that both Law and Gospel remain in effect throughout the believer's life. The definition of the Law was expanded to include the commands of Christ, the law of love. Spener did not distinguish in his theology between justification, which makes the believer righteous, and sanctification, which makes him holy. The forgiveness of sins and the creation of a new person were bound together in perfect coordination. He did not believe that justification was a punctiliar, declaratory act but that it was linear, a steadily continuing condition.

Pietists also emphasized the need for a "born again" Christian experience. Spener and other leaders of the movement used a biological metaphor rather than the legal explanations of justification worked out by Luther. This experiential approach led to a great emotional fervor. Francke encouraged this aspect of pietism by describing Christian experience as "cheerful faith," "warmed hearts," and "great joy." Many of his followers taught that happiness and success would inevitably follow the salvation experience. Revivalism grew from the stress on emotion and conversion. A "plan of salvation" developed that stressed conviction of sin, a penitential struggle, and the dated conversion. This new type of Christianity continues to be very influential in the 20th century. Everyone was expected to move through the same stages of repentance and conversion leading to salvation. Individual differences were lost in the teaching.

Pietism represented a great social concern. Christians must always relate to the society or world around them, but they must try not to absorb its values. In the apostle John's writings the world is identified as an evil, corrupt place, and yet Scripture contains the command of Christ to do His work in the world. The Pietists struggled with this problem by denying many worldly pleasures, by realizing that the kingdom of God was coming, and by serving society in every way they could. Worldly pleasures never held much attraction for Francke or Spener. As a student, Spener led a very spartan life, and later he preached against jewelry, card playing, the theater, and the wearing of fine clothes. He taught his followers to be moderate in drinking and eating. An interesting detail with regard to Pietism's attitudes toward drinking is their use of alcoholic beverages. They did not teach total abstinence but rather condemned

drunkenness and encouraged moderation. One of their industries at Halle was a brewery. But Pietism did teach a kind of
asceticism as reflected in Francke's rules for the Christian life:
"Do not speak much. . . . Trifling jests and anecdotes, do not
become a Christian. When you are in conversation, avoid
speaking of yourself, or desiring so to do. . . . Avoid unnecessary
mirth. . . . If others laugh at foolish jests, and improper
expressions, do not join with them. . . . Engage in no
unprofitable work; for you shall give account of every moment
of your time, and of the manner in which it has been employed.
Read not trifling nor useless books, for the sake of passing away
time."[1]

Pietism was as positive toward some worldly activities as
it was negative toward others. The schools at Halle were
oriented toward more practical activities than were other 17th-
century educational institutions. Pietists encouraged hard
work and demanded self-discipline in following one's calling
or profession. They did not feel that asceticism made an
individual more holy. Rather, Spener taught that the pleasures
of the world would get in the way of service to God and to one's
fellow men.

Spener had high hopes for society because of his belief in
the coming kingdom of God. He did not set a date for the new
age, but he looked for the conversion of the Jews, the destruction of the Roman Catholic Church, and the glorious spread of
God's rule over the whole earth. He believed that the church in
the present age, should be a pilot project for the future, when
Christ returns. Although the complete realization of the
kingdom is yet to come, Christians should anticipate it by
fostering revivals as well as engaging in various social and
philanthropic enterprises.

Pietists promoted efforts to help the poor, free the slaves,
improve the treatment of prisoners, eliminate social class
distinctions, obtain religious liberty, and achieve social justice.
Their teaching led to reduction of drunkenness and to the
moral drive that helped Germany rebuild after the devastation

of the Thirty Years' War. Conversion, they felt, should lead a person to work for the betterment of the world around him. Francke and Spener criticized the actions of the princes. They denounced war as folly and believed that the ruler's power extended over earthly things but cannot extend to a person's conscience. Pietists believed that when a prince tries to control a person's thoughts and religious beliefs he exceeds his authority and need not be obeyed.

EDUCATION AND CHARITABLE INSTITUTIONS

Pietism stimulated a new enthusiasm for education and philanthropy. Spener encouraged the founding of a workhouse in Frankfurt and a number of cities such as Nuernberg, Augsburg, Leipzig, Halle, and Berlin established similar institutions. These institutions were to serve impoverished and unemployed people and force loafers to work. They were also to care for orphans and provide a base for development of new industries. Though they met with limited success, they demonstrated a new and earnest attempt on the part of the church to tackle social problems.

The major leader in pietist education and charity was not Spener, but Francke. The latter's vision of a better world involved not only changes in the church but a reordering of all human institutions in the interest of a more just society for everyone. Francke's work at Halle was meant to be a model for others. He established a new educational system based on a new series of institutions from the university to the folk school. He counted on his students to introduce his reforms elsewhere. Four major types of schools were established at Halle. One was the Paedagogium, in which the sons of nobles were trained for careers in the army and the bureaucracy. A second was the Latin school, where the sons of professional and merchant families were prepared for the university, to become theologians, lawyers, medical doctors, and businessmen. A third, the German school, trained the common people's sons and daughters to become tradespeople and housewives. The fourth was a free institution for poor children.

University students were hired to teach in these schools. The system made it possible for the sons of the poor to attend a university and encouraged the education of the young. The close connection between the university and the lower schools was one of Franke's major innovations. He also relied on education to bridge class distinctions. Sons of middle class people were allowed to study at the Paedagogium, and orphans were admitted to the more prestigious schools. Of 96 orphans, 60 were studying in the Latin school in 1706. Francke placed great emphasis on allowing each student to develop according to his own ability.

The curricula of these schools reflected the Pietist desire that education should be relevant to life. Teachers at the school for the poor were not only to teach reading, writing, and arithmetic but also history, geography, science, and law. The students at the Paedagogium studied Latin, Greek, Hebrew, French, law, medicine, geography, history, science, geometry, music, and speech. They also took nature walks and went on field trips to art studios and workshops. In addition to their academic accomplishments, they had to demonstrate a knowledge of certain basic trades such as carpentry. These educational changes did not depend solely upon a new curriculum, but also upon dedicated, kindly, pious teachers. Many theological students were employed as teachers because they were expected to live as well as study the Christian faith. In 1707 a "Seminary of Preceptors" was founded at Halle as a teacher-training institution. The school featured a five-year course, including two years of humanities and three years of practice teaching and study combined. The main goal of Pietist education was the development of godly character. That meant individuals who were temperate, responsible, concerned for others, honorable, pious, and kindly. Francke did not depend on the harsh discipline used in other schools of his day but wanted children treated with compassion and consideration. On the other hand, he should not be regarded as a 20th-century educator, since he advocated close supervision and control of students. His educational treatise, *Short and Simple Instruction*, indicates that he opposed children's play in any form. He also insisted that young people learn manners appropriate to their place in society. Despite these limitations, Pietist education led to profound changes. No longer was education to be book centered. A school was regarded not only as a place where information was transmitted but also as an institution to transform character. Educational content and method were to be flexible and suited to social needs. Most important, the poor (even destitute orphans) were to be given the opportunity to secure a sound education. By 1727, the Halle schools enrolled 2,300 children and their influence was felt throughout Germany and the rest of the West.

Francke also wished to restructure theological education. The ministry remained the key institution for Pietists in their program for a renewed church and a better society. A constant theme in their approach to theology was the need for an individual to live his beliefs and not only talk about them. A minister was to be a Christian gentleman who lived in a generous, kindly, truthful, friendly, and honest manner. He was to be clean, brave, punctual, and family oriented. Such attitudes were to be developed by a strong devotional life of prayer, Bible reading, and meditation. Piety was also to be accompanied by academic competence. A pastor was to know Latin, Hebrew, and Greek before beginning his theological study. The ministerial course included the study of hermeneutics, exegesis, polemics, church history, and dogmatics. Practical experience was provided for students by assigning them to teach the Christian faith to students in the Halle schools.

Pietist philanthropy as exemplified in the Halle community included much more than education. Francke was interested in supporting orphans whom he began to place in foster homes. In 1696 he bought a house for use as an orphanage. Another home was established in 1698 where widows could live in comfort with medical and spiritual care. The widows were given the task of praying for the church and the rulers. A physician, Christian Richter, donated his property and services to the Halle foundation to establish a medical dispensary. A bookstore was established, with branches throughout Germany. A publishing house was started by Karl Hildebrand, baron von Canstein (1667—1719), a follower of Francke, to print Bibles and other religious literature. This establishment continued from 1710 to 1812 and published nearly 2,500,000 copies of the Scriptures. Many of these Halle industries gave employment to Francke's wards, and the profits from their operations helped to fund his educational and charitable institutions.

FOREIGN MISSIONS

Pietism encouraged the growth of missions. It was Francke who emerged as the leader in this aspect of the movement. His interest in missions began in 1705 when Frederick IV (1671—1730; king of Denmark and Norway 1699—1730) was looking for two men to send as preachers to his colonies. Denmark had a small trading port at Tranquebar, on the southeastern coast of India, and it was the custom to send chaplains there. Frederick became interested in reaching the non-Christians as well as the Christians of the area. When no Danish ministers could be interested in the work, he contacted Francke, who chose two Halle students, Bartholomaeus Ziegenbalg (1683—1719) and Heinrich Pluetschau (ca. 1677/78—ca. 1746/47), to go to India. This was the beginning of the Danish, later the Danish-Halle mission. Despite great hardships and hostility, the early pietist missionaries met with great success.

Their activity set the pattern for many later Protestant missions. The Halle missionaries placed major emphasis on education. Christians must be taught to read, so that they could study the Word of God. This necessitated the building of schools to train the young. If believers were expected to read the

Bible, it had to be translated into their language. Ziegenbalg learned the Tamil language and translated the New Testament into it by 1714. Before he died he also finished rendering the Old Testament into Tamil as far as the Book of Ruth. These early missionaries also insisted that the Gospel be preached in a meaningful manner to Indian audiences. This made it necessary to understand Indian religions and culture. To accomplish this, Ziegenbalg studied Eastern religions and wrote a book that he sent to Europe. His work was not well received and remained unpublished until 1867. Another characteristic of early missionary activity was its insistence on personal conversion. Missionaries did not try to deal with large groups, as the Catholic Asian missions had done, but tried to win individuals to Christ. Finally, the Halle mission tried to create an indigenous church and ministry. As soon as possible there were to be Indian pastors and local churches.

The Danish-Halle work became famous throughout Europe. Letters that missionaries wrote to Francke were published, and he began a newspaper that carried notices about this ministry. He also used his large network of correspondents and personal connections to encourage interest in missions throughout Europe. Many who heard of the Indian mission sent gifts to Halle to support it. No area of Europe was more moved by the cause than England. Missionary letters were translated into English and received broad distribution. When Ziegenbalg was on furlough he visited England, where he was received by the king as well as the Archbishop of Canterbury. This interest was very important for the future of the Indian work. The missionaries had begun to expand their preaching beyond the small Danish settlements into British India and other territories ruled by the independent Kingdom of Tanjore. The Danish king did not wish to have his funds used for evangelizing areas not under his control, and so money was donated by the English. The East India Company had been expanding British influence in the land and had hired chaplains for its personnel as well as for the troops that supported its efforts. Many ministers brought to serve in this capacity were underpaid and inadequate for the task. The situation led the British to use the Halle missionaries as chaplains. An unusual situation developed as German missionaries sent out by the king of Denmark found themselves serving as chaplains to the British and preaching to non-Christians while being supported by the High Church Anglican Society for Promoting Christian Knowledge. These missionaries used the Book of Common Prayer and baptized and observed the Lord's Supper in the Anglican fashion.

Perhaps the most famous of these missionaries was Christian Friedrich Schwartz (1726—98). One of 60 men sent to the foreign fields from Halle during the 18th century, he served in India for 48 years. After spending a decade at Tranquebar, he became chaplain to a British settlement. From 1772 until his death he served in Tanjore, where, in addition to pastoral duties, he was involved in politics. Though he was a brilliant and cultured man who knew several languages, including English, Portugese, Tamil, Persian, and Hindustani, he lived a simple, godly life. Constantly witnessing to the power of the risen Savior, he made a lasting impression on those who met him. Under Schwartz's leadership the Tanjore Church grew to over 2,000 members.

Impressed by the dedication of the missionaries, Francke established a missionary training school at Halle. Under pietist influence Frederick IV established the Royal College for Advancing the Cause of the Gospel to educate and support missionaries. Several ministers were sent to evangelize the Lapps in northern Norway and Sweden. Frederick also gave funds to the Pietist missions of Hans Egede (1686—1758) in Greenland. Egede wished to evangelize the Norwegian settlers of the island, but when he arrived in 1721 he could find no trace of them. Therefore he redirected his efforts to reach the Eskimo residents of Greenland. His work illustrates the trials and frustrations of pioneer effort. He had great difficulty mastering the Eskimo language and found it deficient in terms that could be used to preach the Gospel. The Greenlanders were superstitious and under control of witches who opposed his every move.

He finally won a few individuals to Christ, but for the most part he had to be content to baptize infants in the hope that the younger generation would become Christians. In 1736 he returned to Denmark and continued to direct the Greenland church from there. He published several books that did much to advance the theory of missions. After his death his son Paul carried on the work. Paul wrote an Eskimo dictionary and grammar and translated the New Testament into the Eskimo language.

In 1733 a new mission, sponsored by Moravians, was started in Greenland. The friction between these later arrivals and the Egede group is a sad tale. But the Moravians were very faithful and built a church that has endured in Greenland. Under Zinzendorf's leadership the Moravians became a missionary church. They tended to go to the most remote, neglected, and difficult places. Many of their missionaries were humble people, farmers and craftsmen, whose aim was to live the Gospel as well as witness through words. They went to North America (1734), Lapland and South America (1735), South Africa (1736), Labrador (1791), and Tibet (1856).

Another outstanding missionary influenced by Pietism was Henry Melchior Muehlenberg (1711—87). He was educated at Goettingen and then was a teacher in the Halle orphanage. He was ordained in 1739 and was diaconus and inspector of an orphanage at Grosshennersdorf, Silesia, 1739—41. In 1742 he went as a missionary to Lutheran congregations in Pennsylvania. A man of great vision, he saw unlimited possibilities for expansion in the new field. The demands on his time were so great that he sent to Halle for help. In 1745 men and money arrived for the new work. By 1748 his energetic leadership resulted in the summoning of the first Lutheran Synod in America, the Evangelical Lutheran Ministerium of Pennsylvania. This group supervised the growing number of Lutheran churches in the middle colonies and set the standards for synodical organization in other areas. A man of zeal and organizational ability, Muehlenberg has been aptly named "the father of American Lutheranism."

Jewish evangelism was also an area of Pietist missionary concern. An institute for Jewish studies was opened at Halle in 1728 under direction of Johann Heinrich Callenberg (1694—1760). A former professor at the University of Halle, he had prepared Christian writings in Arabic, Persian, and Turkish so that Muslims could be won to Christ. His interest in Oriental studies led him to a desire to preach the Gospel to the Jews. The Jewish institute prepared Christian literature in Hebrew and sent out several missionaries to work among the Jews. The Moravians were also active in this ministry, and one of their first missionaries, Johann Leonhard Dober (1706—66) spent three years ministering to the Jews in Amsterdam.

HYMNS AND DEVOTIONAL LITERATURE

Pietist hymns and devotional literature reflect many of the same trends found in these forms of expression among Orthodox writers. One of the most influential of Pietist hymnwriters was Joachim Neander (1650—80) of the German Reformed Church. Born at Bremen, he became a teacher at Frankfurt in 1671. In 1674 he became head of the Reformed grammar school at Duesseldorf where he used Spener's idea of organizing small group meetings for worship. Because of this activity he was dismissed. In 1679 he became a pastor at Bremen, where he remained until his death. Neander was not only a teacher and a theologian but also an accomplished poet who wrote more than 60 hymns, which he set to music. The Calvinists did not compose hymns until Neander's time. Early leaders of the group, such as John Calvin and Huldreich Zwingli, had discouraged the use of church choirs, organs, and other forms of ecclesiastical art. Even such hymns as the Lutherans were writing were prohibited because they were the production of men. God was to be worshiped only by the divinely inspired hymns of the psalms. This led to the practice of versifying the psalms, that is, putting them in metrical form so they could be sung.

Neander's work marks a break from the practice of

singing only psalms in the Reformed Church. His hymns have won for him the title of the "Gerhardt of the Reformed Church." His work focuses on praise to God. The joyful tone and smooth flow of his songs caused them to be accepted by Lutherans as well as Reformed. Many of his hymns are odes to nature as well as to nature's God. One of them, "Praise to the Lord, the Almighty," seems to grow in popularity with the years. This hymn, based on Psalms 103 and 150, is quite different from early Calvinistic psalmody. The following two stanzas, in the translation slightly altered by Catherine Winkworth, illustrates the beauty of his work:

Praise to the Lord, the Almighty, the King of creation!
O my soul, praise Him, for He is thy Health and Salvation!
    Join the full throng;
    Wake, harp and psalter and song;
Sound forth in glad adoration. . . .

Praise to the Lord, Oh, let all that is in me adore Him!
All that hath life and breath,
        come now with praises before Him!
    Let the Amen
    Sound from His people again;
Gladly for aye we adore Him.

Gerhard Tersteegen (1697—1769), who came from the German Reformed community and was influenced by Pietism, also wrote many outstanding hymns. His parents wanted him to become a minister, but the death of his father forced him to take an apprenticeship with a shopkeeper at Muelheim. Converted in 1716, he became very popular and was widely admired for his mystical, ascetic life. He left the Reformed Church in 1725 and gave himself to a life of service to others. Through correspondence and personal contacts he influenced Christians in Holland, Scandinavia, and Germany. He wrote over 100 hymns that speak of the mystical presence of God.

Neither Francke nor Spener were hymnwriters, but other Lutheran Pietists produced marvelous songs. Francke's successor as head of the Halle institution, Johann Anastasius

Freylinghausen (1670—1739), became the leading hymnist of the movement. Before coming to Halle, Freylinghausen had studied at the universities at Frankfurt and Jena. At Halle he became Francke's assistant and married his daughter. He taught theology and homiletics, but his greatest contribution was the *Geistreiches Gesangbuch,* which is regarded as the most important collection of Pietist hymns. The first edition was published in 1704 and contained 683 hymns. A second version appeared in 1714, with 815 additional hymns. The two editions were reissued in 1741, enlarged, with 1,582 hymns and 600 tunes. Freylinghausen composed 44 of these hymns and 22 hymn tunes. His hymns are characterized by depth of feeling and a clear understanding of Holy Scripture. His choices of tunes departed from the usual Lutheran chorales and they were often not well suited to congregational worship. Two of his hymns still frequently sung are "Lift Up Your Heads, Ye Mighty Gates," and "O Jesus, Source of Calm Repose."

Karl Heinrich von Bogatzky (1690-1774), a Hungarian nobleman, studied law at Jena and studied theology under Francke at Halle. Because he was too sickly for the pastoral ministry, he helped with the orphanage at Halle. While engaged in this task he wrote the first Pietist missionary hymn, "Awake Thou Spirit."

Some of the first Pietist hymns were written by the Wuerttemberg school, whose leading member was Philipp Friedrich Hiller (1699—1769). A student of Bengel, Hiller was a pastor at Steinheim until he lost his voice in 1751 and was forced to resign. Despite this discouragement, he was a prolific writer and wrote over 1,000 hymns. Hiller's hymns are cast in a simple form and do not engage in the flights of fancy that are often characteristic of the schools of Pietist hymnody.

Moravians also made great contributions to church music and hymnwriting. Zinzendorf wrote over 2,000 hymns—his first when he was 12 years old—and was still composing in the year of his death. John Wesley made the following translation of part of one of Zinzendorf's finest hymns:

> "Jesus, Thy blood and righteousness
> My beauty are, my glorious dress;
> Midst flaming worlds, in these arrayed,
> With joy shall I lift up my head. . . .
> Thou God of power, Thou God of love,
> Let the whole world Thy mercy prove!
> Now let Thy word o'er all prevail;
> Now take the spoils of death and hell."

Orthodox devotional writing found great favor with the Pietists. Spener's *Pia Desideria* was written as an introduction to Johann Arndt's *True Christianity*. Arndt's works continued to be popular among Pietists. Sermons by preachers like Francke were published and widely distributed. Other such collections included those by Hiller and Johann Friedrich Starck (1680—1756), whose *Daily Handbook in Good and Evil Days* was widely used. At first, when there was a lack of Pietist clergymen, the movement spread through devotional literature. It was customary to read a sermon at meetings, and many homes had sermon books, hymnal, and the Bible for their religious library. If the family could not attend church on Sunday, the father would read a sermon to his household.

In 1730 the first German devotional paper, *Spiritual Tidings*, was published in Berleburg, and between 1726 and 1742 the seven-volume Berleburg Bible was published. This was an original translation and a radical pietist exposition of the Scriptures. Tersteegen also wrote much devotional material for Pietists, including the *Selected Biographies of the Saints*. He also translated older mystical books from French and Latin into German.

PIETISM AND THE PRINCES

Many rulers in Protestant Europe were favorable to the Pietist movement. Some of them, such as the counts of Wittgenstein, controlled small areas while others, like the kings of Prussia, ruled over major territories. In 1709 Francke was invited to Berlin to advise Frederick I (1657—1713; king of

Prussia 1701—13) in the establishment of new state charities including an orphanage. Frederick William I (1688—1740; king of Prussia 1713—40), inspired by Pietism, founded an orphans' home for the children of his soldiers in 1722.

Perhaps the most obvious example of the affect of Pietism on the princes was the influence the movement had on the Prussian school system. Many wealthy citizens and princes were led by the example of Francke to become interested in founding educational institutions. The most important of these was Frederick William I of Prussia. In 1717 he issued a decree demanding that children between the ages of 5 and 16 attend school, and he set up 2,000 new schools to provide for them. The pupils were to go to school daily in the winter, and at least once a week in the summer so that they would not forget all they learned in the winter. Seminaries were established under Pietist direction to train teachers for these schools. It was on the foundation of these Pietist type schools that the later Prussian educational system was established. The close association of the princes with Pietism prepared the way for the transference of religious sentiment to the growing national states. The Christian patriotism of the 19th and 20th centuries developed from 18th-century currents, such as Pietism.

5.

Enlightenment, Revolution, and Christianity

THE IMPACT OF MODERN SCIENCE ON RELIGION

The development of modern science led to many changes in the intellectual outlook of the 18th century. The new approach, called the Enlightenment, grew from leadership of individuals who wished to apply the ideas of Isaac Newton (1642—1727) to religion and society. The leaders of this movement were brilliant Frenchmen called philosophers or philosophes. The attitudes of the philosophes spread to other lands and included such writers as Benjamin Franklin (1706—90), Thomas Jefferson (1743—1826), Joseph Priestley (1733—1804), and David Hume (1711—76). As exponents of the scientific world view they used many literary forms and wrote in such brilliant style that they made even the most dry and abstract subjects interesting.

The most famous philosophe was Francois Marie Arouet, who took the name Voltaire (1694—1778). Born to a middle class family of moderate wealth, as a young man he offended a noble by some of his writings and was forced to flee to England. He enjoyed freedom of expression there and also became acquainted with the ideas of Newton and John Locke (1632—1704). Convinced that the world was a great machine run by natural laws, he devoted the rest of his life to demonstrating this to others. He returned to France and wrote essays, dramas, novels, and poetry to spread his teaching. Because his work threatened traditional religion, he found it necessary to live just across the border in Switzerland. Though he was the friend of aristocrats, princes, and kings, he never abandoned his views of social justice for all men based on the laws of nature and nature's God.

Another important philosophe, Denis Diderot (1713—84), tried to publicize the new scientific outlook through a great encyclopedia. This work, which appeared in 28 volumes between the years 1751 and 1772, was more than a mere collection of facts. It declared that man could improve himself if he replaced faith with reason as his guiding principle. Such teaching constituted a threat to every form of established authority. Because of this, the earlier volumes of the work were suppressed, but by the time the last one appeared, the *Encyclopedia* had triumphed over intolerance and could be openly distributed. Diderot was determined to make useful knowledge widely available. He assured the high quality of his work by securing articles from over 130 experts and writers, a veritable Who's Who of 18th-century talent that included Voltaire, Rousseau (1712—78), and the famous mathematician Jean Le Rond d'Alembert (ca. 1717—83). A unique feature of the *Encyclopedia* was its eleven volumes of illustrations. The 3,000 pages of pictures had a tremendous impact. Many of them helped doctors and scientists. The industrial diagrams showed craftsmen how to do everything from making rope to weaving lace step-by-step. The work also contained implied criticisms of existing ideas and institutions. The article on the goddess Juno criticized the cult of the Virgin Mary, the article on salt discussed the injustice to the poor of taxes on necessities, and the article on Geneva condemned the French government.

The religious view expounded by the philosophes was deism, an outlook similar to what would today be called Unitarianism. Deism had been elaborated during the 17th century. In some respects it was a resumption of the religious humanism of Renaissance men like Desiderius Erasmus (ca. 1466—1536) and Thomas More (1478—1535). In contrast to the view of the Reformation that regarded natural man and his culture as basically evil, the humanists were optimistic about man and the world. Many 17th- and 18th-century writers adopted the humanists' outlook and tried to establish a religion that would be a base for the entire range of cultural activities. They believed in an ethical god and were moved to reverence and worship by the order of nature and the capacity of man. These ideas were opposed to orthodox Christian teachings about salvation and the Holy Scriptures, but these men did not at first attack Christianity. They rather tried to work within the church, trying to liberalize theology and to redirect the energies of Christians.

The earliest expression of deism is *De veritate (On the Truth),* by Edward Herbert, better known as Baron Herbert of Cherbury (1583—1648). An Oxford-trained soldier, diplomat, and philosopher, he opposed all special revelation on the ground that it corrupted the purity of natural religion by introducing conflict and superstition where originally there had been agreement and truth. He contended that the following ideas are common to all religions: (1) the existence of a supreme being, (2) the need to worship the supreme being, (3) the importance of virtue and piety for worship, (4) the necessity of repentance, and (5) the future life of rewards and punishments. Whenever human beings rely on reason, he felt, they recognize the validity of these ideas. He believed that deism was the teaching of the one true church, which existed before people were misled by the priests and prophets of the various religions. He also taught that the rites and doctrines of institutional religion had caused the most savage persecutions.

Herbert's ideas found a fertile ground in 18th-century Europe because geographical expansion had widened knowledge of other faiths. During the Middle Ages, Christendom seemed to stand at the center of history, but when traders and missionaries returned to Europe with stories of hundreds of millions of Chinese and Indians who had never heard of Christ, it seemed that Christian history only applied to one minority movement. The worship of nature and nature's god (natural theology) seemed to offer a solution to this problem.

But something had happened to natural theology. The scientific revolution had developed a mechanistic and materialistic view of the universe. Because of the control this outlook gave over the forces of nature, the abstractions of the mathematicians were increasingly believed to be true. The theology built on this description of the universe turned out to be less suited to the world view of the Bible than the medieval outlook had been. Against the mechanical regularity of the new science the Biblical miracles seemed irrational. Time and space had exploded to such vast dimensions as to dwarf the Christian account of history, which extended from creation to the Last Judgment. Deism seemed to offer a way to be religious and adjust to the new scientific world view.

During the first half of the 18th century in England, deist and orthodox theologians debated over miracles and the Old Testament prophecies of Christ. The deists lost the battle. The defenders of Christianity demonstrated a vitality in their faith not found in natural religion freed of revelation. Upon closer scrutiny, deism turned out to be a collection of ideas rather than a living faith. David Hume's *Dialogues on Natural Religion* pointed out that the deists assumed everything that needed to be proved and logically had no better case than orthodox theology. Another writer condemned the entire attempt to put forward rational proof for religion, stating that the validity of the Christian faith rested on an inner experience with God. What happened in England was that the best minds showed deism to be an untenable stopping point. The real choice was between Christianity and skepticism. Those who wished to remain Christian tended to join the Wesleyan revival. Others, inclined toward skepticism, turned away from religion to other activities they considered more useful.

While the debate died out in England, it was renewed with vigor in France. The chief spokesman for French rationalism was Voltaire. He was more capable than the English deists, and the church in France had few able defenders. Indeed, French Catholicism was so inflexible that it gave little hope to those who desired change. Voltaire felt he had identified man's problems, namely, priestly exploitation, superstition, intolerance, and persecution. He continued to express his hope to see the last king strangled in the bowels of the last priest.

Advocates of deism could also be found in Germany. Hermann Samuel Reimarus (1694—1768) defended natural religion and rejected miracles. He believed that the miraculous element was introduced into Scripture because of the fanaticism and deceit of the Biblical writers. The great miracle of revelation, according to Reimarus, is the world, and in nature one can find God, morality, and immortality. Gotthold Ephraim Lessing (1729—81) put forth his rationalistic ideas in two major works, *Nathan the Wise* and *The Education of the Human Race.* The former is a play about a tolerant Jew who regards all religions as equally valid ways to moral perfection. The second places mankind in the third of three stages of education. The first represented childhood and was the Old Testament with its laws enforced by rewards and punishments. Next was the youth stage under the New Testament with its ideals of self-surrender and sacrifice. The present, or adult, stage is based on reason. Lessing thus held that the guidelines of the Bible were childish and that those of reason were mature.

The German rationalists were answered by one of the most profound philosophers Western society has produced, Immanuel Kant (1724—1804). His ideas set in motion trends that scholars still investigate. Kant was a professor at the Prussian University of Koenigsberg. Educated as a Pietist, he sought to combine rationalism and orthodox Christianity. In such works as the *Critique of Pure Reason* he stated that science and reason do not provide proof of the existence of God, moral law, and immortality. Science, he believed, describes the physical world but cannot provide a guide for morality. There are, however, human experiences, such as awareness of beauty, conscience, and religious feeling, whose reality cannot be doubted, though science has difficulty dealing with them. These instincts are planted by God to teach people good and evil. Kant called this awareness the "categorical imperative." It forces humans to choose between right and wrong. His insistence that science is limited, and that moral truth comes in a different way than scientific knowledge, refuted the naive rationalism of the philosophes.

THE IMPACT OF MODERN SCIENCE ON SOCIETY

The philosophes also wished to apply Newtonian science to society. They believed that there were natural laws that regulated the universe and human society. Acting on this assumption, they applied reason to social institutions and traditions. These attempts led them to express the idea of progress, an outlook that has continued until the 20th century. Their optimism received its most forceful expression in the work of the Marquis de Condorcet (1743—94). His *Sketch for a Historical Picture of the Progress of the Human Mind* predicted that mankind was destined for unlimited progress in all fields because it had found and applied the method of human reason to arrive at truth.

The society to which the philosophes began to apply reason, France during the Ancien Regime, was in a very traditional, irrational situation. Programs for revitalizing social life included suggestions for economics, religion and law, and government. In economics they wished to see the doctrine of laissez-faire applied. This meant that people should be able to do as they wished without government control over their economic activities. The most famous expression of laissez-faire, *Inquiry into the Nature and Causes of the Wealth of Nations,* by Adam Smith (1723—90), argued that individuals are motivated by self-interest in economics and that if each person pursues his own path, the good of the entire society will be served.

The religious views of the philosophes have already been discussed, but there were also some social implications of their ideas. Writers of the Enlightenment linked their desire for religious change with a demand for toleration. They pointed out that it is foolish and immoral to force a person to accept ideas opposed to his or her conscience. Intolerance is an affront to the Christian teaching of love. Faith is a matter of individual concern over which society should have no control. One form that the philosophe campaign for religious liberty took was an attack on bigoted religious laws. Voltaire led the way in this work with his involvement in the Calas case. Jean Calas (1698—1762), a Protestant of Toulouse, was accused of murdering his son and was executed. He was believed to have murdered his son because the latter intended to become Catholic. The execution of Calas enraged Voltaire, who set out on a campaign to clear the man's name. His efforts were to take three years and involve the writing of many pamphlets and the collection of a legal defense fund. Voltaire looked over the court record, made enquiries, and concluded that young Calas was mentally disturbed and had committed suicide. His unrelenting demands led the courts to declare Calas innocent and to dismiss the judge responsible for that miscarriage of justice.

The philosophe campaign against religious laws led to an insistence on a more rational and humane approach to other victims of 18th-century justice. Slavery, inhuman treatment of the insane, and the torture of prisoners—all came under attack.

An Italian philosophe, Cesare Beccaria (1738—94), wrote *Crimes and Punishments*, which argued for the application of reason to criminal justice. Laws, he wrote, were to be fair and clearly stated. The aim of punishment was not to be vengeance but the prevention of further crime. The penalty should fit the offense; justice was to be speedy; torture and capital punishment were to be abolished. The state should reward good deeds and educate people about the dangers of a life of crime. Beccaria's work led to penal reform in many areas of Europe.

Most of the Enlightenment programs for a better society involved a change in government. It was assumed that people are by nature basically good, rational, and capable of being educated. If natural laws were discovered and explained to people, they would follow them and form societies that would maximize human happiness. The philosophes felt that oppressive social, political, and economic institutions were the creations of scheming rulers and priests. Society was to be organized for the benefit of all its members, not just for the good of a ruling elite. Although they thought in terms of states, their belief in rationality led to a cosmopolitan outlook. With the triumph of natural law a united and uniform world civilization would emerge in which all nations would cooperate.

Political thinkers of the Enlightenment followed John Locke (1632—1704) in assuming that governments started when men formed contracts with rulers to protect individual rights. They argued that citizens may revolt against the government if it fails in its duty. But most philosophes did not support democratic or representative government. They felt the nation could function best if controlled by the absolute rule of an enlightened despot aided by a group of educated men who would establish freedom of thought and promote educational and material progress.

Some of the rulers of 18th-century Europe tried to fill the role outlined for them by the philosophes. The most famous of these enlightened despots were Frederick the Great (1712—86; king of Prussia 1740—86), Catherine the Great (1729—96; empress of Russia 1762—96), and Joseph II (1741—90; Holy Roman emperor 1765—90). Such leaders adopted more benevolent programs because in large measure their own interests could be served by the application of reason to their states. Great prosperity would increase the amount that could be taxed, and more efficient administration could strengthen the central government's control. Each of the rulers followed a similar pattern of change and reform. Agricultural techniques were improved, laws were rationalized, torture was stopped, and public health was improved through the construction of hospitals and asylums. Enlightened despots supported scholarship and tried to raise the educational level of the populace. Religious tolerance was established, and the Catholic countries restrained papal influence in their lands. But though they were sincere, these rulers had little success. The clergy and nobles opposed the reforms and persuaded the successors of the enlightened rulers to restore the old ways.

The most sophisticated of the philosophe political theorists was Charles de Secondat, baron de Montesquieu (1689—1755). Unlike the other philosophes, he did not support the enlightened despots, nor did he believe that all people were alike. A French noble, he opposed royal absolutism as much for its inefficiency as for its tyranny. His *Persian Letters* used the form of letters written by two Persian travelers in Europe to satirize the social, political, and religious institutions of the age. The book attacked the Roman Catholic Church for its dogmas of transubstantiation and the Trinity and accused the church of committing a host of crimes and atrocities.

In 1726 Montesquieu set out on a long European tour to discover for himself what conditions existed in other lands. The trip took him to England, where he was deeply impressed by the British governmental system. Returning to France, he spent many years writing his masterpiece, *The Spirit of the Laws*. This book used a comparative technique to discover the fundamental principles of politics. He claimed there were three types of government: republics, monarchies, and despotisms. The form of a state varied according to its natural environment and history. Republics, he believed, flourished in small countries, monarchies in moderate sized areas located in the temperate zone, and despotisms in large empires in the hot climates.

He urged France to emulate the English and establish a separation of powers that would safeguard liberty. In England, he thought, the executive, legislative, and judicial branches were separate and checked and balanced one another. Actually, Montesquieu misunderstood England, because the Revolution of 1688 (or Glorious Revolution) had led to the supremacy of Parliament in the land. Nevertheless, his analysis made the tripartite division of government the model for liberals who wanted to protect individual freedom. It had great effect on those who drafted the American Constitution in 1787 and on others who drew up constitutions in other lands during the 19th century. Although Montesquieu continued to attack Roman Catholicism by condemning intolerance and clerical celibacy, he admitted that Christianity was a powerful moral force in society because it generated order and happiness.

A more radical exception to the general philosophe outlook is in the work of Jean Jacques Rousseau (1712—78). Although he began as a loyal son of the Enlightenment, Rousseau gave expression to the romantic movement, which was destined to replace rationalism as the major outlook of Western civilization. Born in a turbulent working-class section of Geneva, he ran away from home at the age of 16 and always felt alienated from society despite his fame. Rousseau's own unhappy life probably shaped his view of the world. In his writings he held that individuals in a natural state are fundamentally good, for nature is characterized by a warmth of feeling and love for others. But progress and growth of civilization corrupts people. The main enemy of a state of nature is the introduction of private property. Rousseau claimed that the good qualities of mankind stem from emotion, and the evil habits come from reason. Therefore intuition and emotion are far better guides to conduct than philosophy and reason. In *New Heloise* and *Emile* he described an educational program that would enable people to preserve their innate feelings for virtue and justice.

In *The Social Contract* he devised a government that would preserve as far as possible the natural equality of man. He stated that all citizens, when they agree to form a government, force their individual wills into the general will and agree to accept the decisions of the "general will." If individuals try to place what they believe to be their own interests above the general will, inequalities and injustice result. Those who try to do this must be forced to obey the general will. Rousseau did not explain the mechanisms for carrying out his policies, nor did he realize that forcing a person to behave according to the general will could lead to the denial of individual freedom and the most vicious form of tyranny. His *Social Contract* has been an extremely ambiguous legacy. It has been used to justify both democracy and totalitarianism.

The social ideas of the Enlightenment set the stage for political revolutions. These teachings were subversive of traditional institutions and practices. They presented a challenge not only to France and other European states but also to overseas lands. Philosophe criticisms claimed to be based on universal laws that applied equally to people in America as well as in Europe.

THE AMERICAN REVOLUTION

The first new state founded on principles of the Enlightenment was begun in America. The revolution that led to the American Republic grew from a series of conflicts between the English and the French during the 17th and 18th centuries. These wars (sometimes called the second hundred years' war) involved not only Europe but also the colonial world. They resulted in the triumph of the British in North America and India. The American colonies had contributed little in either men or money to the victory. The war had been won by British soldiers and taxes. When peace came, the English decided that the colonies should make a greater contribution to defense costs. The efforts of the British government to collect taxes for this purpose led to the alienation of the colonists and to the War of Independence.

Religion also helped to bring on the crisis. Many colonial pastors supported the resistance to Britain. With few exceptions the Baptists, Congregationalists, and Presbyterians were ardent champions of the revolution. Efforts of Anglicans to establish a diocese in the colonies frightened many colonial ministers. A series of joint meetings of Congregationalists and Presbyterians made it clear that to them episcopacy was the ecclesiastical tool of absolute government. Government, they taught, was based on a compact or contract between the ruler and the citizens. Many Anglicans, especially those in southern colonies, joined in the protest against an American bishop. In fact, two thirds of the signers of the Declaration of Independence were members of the Church of England.

But other sincere colonial Christians opposed the revolution. These included Anglicans in New England and in the Middle Colonies as well as Methodists. John Wesley wrote very critically of the revolution, and many members of his church followed these views. He believed that the revival that had spread in America was stifled by materialism, which caused the revolution. Also, Wesley agreed with the Lutheran teaching of the duty of passive resistance to constituted authority. Another group that opposed the conflict was composed of pacifists, such as the Quakers, the Church of the Brethren, the Moravians, and the Mennonites. During the fighting these peace churches were misunderstood and persecuted by both sides.

The series of provocative British actions that led to the colonial revolt included mercantilist measures designed to favor other parts of the empire and the imposition of new taxes on the Americans. Most colonial leaders had come to accept the philosophe teaching of free trade, and the new measures seemed anachronistic to them. An example of the ill-advised English moves was the Stamp Act of 1765. The new tax, which was to be levied on every printed paper and legal document, came at a time of depression and raised the question of the right of Parliament to tax the colonies. Since no American representatives sat in Parliament, it was argued that this was taxation without representation. The Stamp Act was repealed as a result of problems in collecting the money and of a boycott of English goods by the colonists. As soon as this crisis passed, the Townshend Acts levied a new series of duties on tea, glass, paper, and other miscellaneous goods. Riots occurred in Boston, and five colonists were shot down by British troops.

In 1770 all the duties were repealed except those on tea. The resistance to even this token of authority led to the dumping of tea into the Boston Harbor in 1773—the Boston Tea Party. The king, angered by the illegal action, closed the port of Boston and changed the constitution of Massachusetts. Many attempts to tighten economic control over the colonies had been accompanied by increased judicial and political power of the crown. American pastors were upset by the injustice of the British move. But in 1774 they received an even more severe shock in the Quebec Act, which gave broad power to the Roman Catholic Church in that area. The act also closed off immigration from New York, Pennsylvania, and Virginia into the Ohio country.

In September 1774 the first Continental Congress met in Philadelphia and challenged Parliament's right to control the colonies. Shortly before a second meeting of the Congress, a skirmish between the Massachusetts militia and the British army at Lexington Green and Concord Bridge (April 19, 1775) opened the hostilities. The colonists felt they were defending their rights as free people. In their challenge to Parliament and the English king they took the first steps in the direction of both republicanism and the equality of man. The philosophes' ideas were taking root in the new world. As relations with the English deteriorated and as the need for European allies became apparent, the Declaration of Independence was adopted by the Continental Congress (July 4, 1776). With French aid and under leadership of General George Washington the fighting began to turn in the colonists' favor. A sizeable force of French infantry and a French fleet cooperating with the Americans enabled Washington to force Britain's largest army in America to surrender at Yorktown in 1781. In the Treaty of Paris (1783) Britain recognized the independence of the colonies.

The instability of the new nation under the Articles of Confederation worried the more wealthy classes, who felt the need for a stronger central government. Their concern led to the Constitutional Convention, which met in Philadelphia in 1787. Out of this meeting came the American Constitution, which went into effect in 1789, creating a federal republic, with certain powers reserved to the states and others given to the central government. The states under this system were more than administrative units of a central bureaucracy. The Constitution also utilized Montesquieu's idea of the separation of powers into the legislative, executive, and judicial branches, with checks and balances built into the governmental mechanism. The judiciary was unique in its power to interpret the constitutionality of the action of the states and the Congress. George Washington (1732—99), a respected leader of high moral standards, was the first president of the Republic (1789—97).

The Constitution forbade the use of religious tests for office holders and guaranteed that there would be no established religion. The Bill of Rights (the first 10 amendments to the Constitution) provided in Amendment I:

> Congress shall make no law respecting an establishment of religion, or prohibiting the free exercise thereof; or abridging the freedom of speech, or of the press, or the right of the people peaceably to assemble, and to petition the Government for a redress of grievances.

The Constitution reflects the movement for religious liberty that had prevailed in Virginia. Just before national independence, James Madison (1751—1836) and Thomas Jefferson (1743—1826) had led a campaign, supported by Presbyterians and Baptists, that had resulted in religious freedom in the colony. The Middle Colonies had already adopted the same solution. In New England the established Congregationalism held on for a generation after independence, but it also gave way before the rationalism of the Enlightenment and the revivalist churches. The United States of America began its history with a religious life shaped by a free church Protestant denominationalism.

The American Revolution has had a profound effect on other peoples. During the 18th century the establishment of an independent republic in America was widely interpreted by Europeans as proving that the ideas of the philosophes could be put into practice. The United States demonstrated that it was possible for a people to set up a government based on the rights of the individual.

THE FRENCH REVOLUTION

The ideas of the Enlightenment that were given concrete

form by the American Revolution provided a model of freedom for Europeans. Frenchmen who had fought in the War of Independence, and the French financial crisis brought on by the expense of supporting the Americans, contributed to the outbreak of the French Revolution. This movement, which was an attempt to realize in Europe many of the achievements of the American government, was to have a greater impact on history than the American Revolution. It brought more social and economic changes and influenced a larger portion of the globe. It also marked the triumph of the middle class (bourgeoisie) and the awakening of the common man, a phenomenon that civilization is still struggling with.

The gross inefficiency of the French government of the 18th century (the Ancien Regime) was another reason for the upheaval. Although France was the center of philosophe thought, it had never been ruled by an enlightened despot. Its social and governmental organization was based on aristocratic privilege, with the population divided into three "estates" or orders, each of which had different legal rights. The first estate was the clergy. The second was the nobility. The third, which included everyone else, had some 20 million peasants and 4 million artisans and middle class in it, out of a total French population of 24.5 million. The first two estates, only 2 percent of the population, owned 35 percent of the land and were exempt from taxation. The tax burden was borne by the third estate and fell most heavily on the peasants, who made up 80 percent of the population. Economic factors were not as important in the alienation of the middle class from the government, because many of them were improving their lot, but they resented the social advantages of the nobility and the exclusion of the bourgeois from the better positions in the army, the church, and the bureaucracy. The middle class wanted political power and social standing to match their economic gains.

The Revolution, which came as a reaction to this inefficient and unjust system, began in 1787 as an aristocratic movement, but it became progressively more radical, until a reaction set in under Napoleon (1769—1821). The French government had been centralized under the king during the 17th century, and noble governors had been replaced by the royal bureaucracy. When Louis XVI (1754—93; king of France 1774—92) found himself in financial difficulties because of heavy expenses in support of the American Revolution, the nobles tried to regain power. In 1787, when the government tried to levy a uniform property tax, regardless of the social status of the owner, the aristocrats demanded that the national parliament, the Estates-General, be assembled. The group had not met since 1614, but the nobles insisted that such a sweeping tax change could not be made without the consent of the entire nation through its representative assembly. The king finally agreed that the Estates-General was convened in 1789. The nobles assumed that they could control the body, but they were wrong. The meeting unleashed a revolutionary storm that destroyed the ruling institutions of France.

The Estates-General that met did not represent the people but rather the three orders of French society. The third estate proved to be the most dynamic group and gave leadership to the meeting. Some of the clergy chose to vote with the third estate as did certain noblemen such as the Marquis de Lafayette (1757—1834). The middle class representatives gained power because they had the money the crown needed, and they had in mind what France should become, namely, a state based upon the principles put forth by the philosophes. The bourgeois succeeded in getting the Estates-General transformed into the National Assembly, with a new voting procedure that gave them control. At first the king resisted the change, but later he agreed to it. But he feared the assembly and brought several regiments of loyal troops to Versailles. It seemed that he would use force to dissolve the group, but the assembly was saved by an uprising of the lower-class people of Paris.

The masses who now threatened the royal establishment were not composed solely of illiterate, unemployed people. They were groups under leadership of shopkeepers and managers of small industries. These individuals led the demonstrations and kept the masses informed about the actions of the government. Mobs streamed into the streets demanding food and a just economic program for France. On July 14, 1789, they stormed the Bastille, an ancient fortress symbol of the old regime. The Parisian masses were henceforth to be continually involved in the revolution. Violence spread to the countryside when the peasants, inflamed by news of the Bastille's fall, seized lands, tore down fences, and burned manor houses. Faced with this critical situation, the National Assembly voted an end to feudalism. Legal class differences were eliminated, church lands were confiscated, and the Declaration of the Rights of Man and of the Citizen, a sweeping statement of human rights, was passed. Summed up in the words "Liberty, Equality, and Fraternity," the French achievement was to spread throughout the world. The Paris mobs forced the king to accept its decisions and to move his family to Paris, where he became a virtual prisoner.

The monarchy was powerless, but other nobles, determined to regain their lost privileges and property, secured foreign aid against the new government. There was also a party within the National Assembly that wanted war in order to establish revolutionary regimes in other countries. Conflict began in 1792, with Austria and Prussia fighting France. At first the French were defeated, but later they recovered and drove back the Austrian-Prussian forces. The war led to the dethroning of the king and to the election of a National Convention by universal male suffrage. In 1793 Britain, Holland, and Spain joined the war against France, but by 1795 all enemy armies were defeated by the revolutionary troops. A draft army, inspired by love of country and led by able young generals who had risen from the ranks, proved successful.

The pressure of war led the National Convention to become more radical. The Committee of Public Safety became the dominant force in the government. This group managed the fighting, encouraged the people to heroic action, conducted foreign policy, and ruthlessly crushed opposition through a reign of terror. Thousands charged with treason or other offenses against the government were guillotined. The king (Louis XVI) and queen were guillotined 1793, and then the terror got out of control. One after another of the revolutionary leaders were executed. The terror frightened the middle class. They were also worried about the growing radicalism of the common people, who demanded government regulations of prices and wages, a more just distribution of land, and a social security system. The lower classes had to be brought under control, so that the bourgeois gains of the revolution could be kept. This was done first by a Directory of five (1795) and then by Napoleon (1799).

Napoleon Bonaparte was a Corsican-born artillery officer who became an extremely successful leader of the revolutionary armies. He overthrew the Directory and governed France as First Consul (1799—1804) and then as Emperor (1804—14). Napoleon introduced many domestic reforms that had the effect of making the revolutionary changes permanent. He also made war with most of Europe. This caused a nationalistic reaction among the other states against France. Napoleon's domestic policies have much in common with the moves made by the enlightened despots of the 18th century. He tried to rationalize the French government by codifying laws, centralizing the administration, setting up a national school system, and reaching an agreement with the papacy on church-state relations in France. Napoleon was sympathetic with religion and wanted to establish tolerance among rival faiths. Wherever he extended his control, the Inquisition was abolished and religious freedom was given to minorities. Most French people welcomed the Napoleonic settlement after years of revolutionary turmoil.

But Napoleon's more positive achievements were eclipsed by his war record. His military genius enabled him to extend his control over much of Europe. The areas that were not under direct French supervision were reduced to satellite states. Very little remained outside Napoleon's empire except Britain and Russia. In all the conquered territories he implemented the basic reforms of the French Revolution. These included the abolition of feudal privileges and serfdom, the recognition of the equality of all citizens, and the institution of the Code Napoleon. Many middle class people in the conquered lands appreciated the progressive French regime and the more honest and efficient government that it brought. But as time went on, most subject people became disgusted with French control of their lands. Napoleon's rule was progressive, but it was a foreign rule imposed by force. The people of Europe were becoming nationalistic, and their nationalism came as a result of resistance to the French. This explains the armed revolt in Spain that weakened French strength and the growing opposition in Germany. In 1812, when Napoleon invaded Russia, the people of all classes united to resist him. Russian military strength, combined with the bitter winter, led to the defeat of his Grand Army. Forced to retreat to France, Napoleon abdicated and was exiled to the island of Elba in 1814. He returned to France in 1815 and tried to lead his people to victory but was defeated at Waterloo and exiled again. Napoleon was defeated by the very forces he encouraged. The people who rose against him were those who had been awakened by the teaching of "Liberty, Equality, and Fraternity" and had then turned against the French when they failed to live up to their revolutionary principles.

CHRISTIANITY IN A REVOLUTIONARY AGE

The French Revolution and the forces it unleashed constituted a serious threat for most forms of Christianity. The early stages of the upheaval were accomplished with the cooperation of the lower clergy, i.e., the parish priests. These men broke with the upper class, who held the high posts in the ecclesiastical system and voted with the third estate. The National Assembly showed its respect for these priests by paying their salaries though church taxes and land holdings were abolished. The lower clergy favored the new arrangement because they were given higher salaries. In 1790 the Assembly passed the Civil Constitution of the Clergy, which completely subordinated the church to the state. When certain clergymen protested, a resolution was passed stating that all ministers had to take an oath to obey the constitution. Many clergy refused. The pope declared that all who swore allegiance to the French government were heretical and gave them 40 days to recant. Earlier the papacy had condemned the Declaration of the Rights of Man and of the Citizen and had officially aligned Roman Catholicism with absolutism and aristocracy.

In 1792 France was attacked by Prussia and Austria. In the desperate struggle that followed many Frenchmen came to feel that Pius VI (1717—99; pope 1775—99) was the moving spirit behind the enemy coalition. Action was taken against priests who would not support the revolutionary cause, and they were given 15 days to emigrate. Many were robbed, beaten, and lynched, but about 40,000 managed to escape. They became for the most part propagandists against the French government. The National Convention, which came to power in 1792, had a favorable attitude toward religion and in 1793 proclaimed religious liberty. But an uprising, led by antirevolutionary clergy, changed the Convention's attitude. This led to a great persecution of the church and the establishment of a religion of reason (in reality a worship of the state) in France.

A civil religion had been developing in the land since the early days of the Revolution. In 1790 Bastille Day (July 14) was celebrated throughout France in a very religious fashion. An oath was taken to the country, often around an altar in the open air, and generally preceded by a Catholic religious service. The Christian holidays were deemphasized, and special observances were held to honor nature or pagan symbols. By 1793 Christianity was equated with counterrevolution, and the Committee of Public Safety recommended the elimination of all vestiges of the faith, including Sundays and saints days. Christianity was replaced by the "Cult of Reason." Churches were converted into "Temples of Reason." The Virgin and the saints were replaced by revolutionary heroes, such as Rousseau and Voltaire. The new religious movement was inaugurated by the famous ceremony at Notre Dame in Paris, where the statue of the Virgin was replaced by an actress to whom hymns were sung. Some 2,000 towns turned their churches into temples of reason, and many rural parishes followed the example. Foreign countries charged the revolutionary government with being antireligious, so it tried to meet their criticisms by officially sanctioning the worship of a supreme being. The new religion was introduced in June 1794 at a formal ceremony modeled after the mass.

A revised calendar was introduced to replace the old church year. September 22, 1792, the day of the establishment of the Republic, was designated as the beginning of Year 1. The year was divided into 12 months of 30 days, with each of the months named for seasonal characteristics. Every 10th day was to be a time of rest. In 1806, when Napoleon abandoned the new calendar, few regretted his move. Additional actions taken against the church at the time the calendar was changed included the suspension of the payment of clerical salaries and a prohibition against priests serving as teachers in the schools. A system of public schools organized throughout France became the center for inculcating civil religion.

Under the Directory (1795—99) there was more religious liberty, and with the rise of Napoleon to power (1799—1814) conditions improved noticeably for the church. Napoleon had several reasons for desiring better relations with the Roman Catholic Church. These included his convictions that France was fundamentally Catholic, that reconciliation with the church would help him achieve his plans, and that people require the authority of revealed religion to achieve happiness. He arranged the 1801 Concordat with the papacy, which recognized Roman Catholicism in France and provided that the clergy would be paid by the state. The Organic Articles of 1802, attached to the Concordat without papal consent, declared that Napoleon could act as he saw fit for the advancement of France. The pope protested in vain the addition of this statement. In 1804 Pius VII (1742—1823; pope 1800—23) assisted at Napoleon's coronation, but later, when he refused to cooperate, the pontiff was deported to France and imprisoned. The pope responded by excommunicating Napoleon.

The struggle between the revolutionary forces and the Christian faith had profound implications for the future. Nationalist religion was to be a major challenge to Christianity in the modern age. Until the Enlightenment and the revolutionary era, people had not thought in terms of the nation. When medieval men identified themselves it was as Christians or as residents of a certain region and only incidentally as Englishmen or Frenchmen. The growth of vernacular languages, the breakup of the Catholic Church into national churches, and the development of dynastic states prepared the way for the new ideology. By the time of the French Revolution, nationalism took on its modern form. The nation was believed to be composed of citizens who lived in a common territory, had a voice in the government, and felt that they had a common heritage and similar interests. During the era of the French Revolution, citizens were required to learn French and attend a network of public schools that emphasized love of country. Many newspapers, periodicals, and pamphlets were published that received wide distribution and tended to draw the nation together. Rites and symbols of nationalism were inaugurated, such as the flag, a national anthem, and special holidays.

These developments caused patriotism to compete with the church for the loyalty of the masses. The total demands of the modern state proved difficult to reconcile with obedience to God. Even in the American Republic, where the government never took the radical antireligious position found in France, nationalism has tended to become a rival to Christianity or to distort the Christian message. An early example of this is in the work of Timothy Dwight (1752—1817). An influential minister, scholar, and writer, Dwight was president of Yale from 1795 to 1817. Much of what he said and did was aimed at stemming the tide of infidelity, which he felt had been started in France with the philosophes, such as Voltaire and the Encyclopedists. Dwight taught that the attitudes of the philosophes had led to the excesses of the French Revolution. Since America also had experienced a revolution, it seemed necessary to exonerate the new world upheaval by showing that the French situation was different. He felt that the prophetic books of the Bible could be used in the situation because it was possible to extend the identification of papal France to republican France. Demonstrating that the French Revolution fulfilled some of the more disreputable prophetic symbols would discredit any extension of its ideals to the United States.

Dwight believed that the forces opposed to true Christianity had been led by the Roman Catholic Church, but that in his day these antichristian elements were being defeated. But as Rome declined, several new teachers of false and immoral doctrines appeared. These new opponents of Christianity were the philosophes, such as Voltaire, Diderot, D'Alembert, and the other contributors to the Encyclopedia. Celebrated for their wit and brilliance, these individuals hated Christianity and were trying to destroy it by replacing it with atheism and irreligion. They had, for example, infiltrated Masonic societies in France and Germany, making these groups centers for the discussion of Enlightenment ideas. The philosophe movement must not be allowed to spread in America, Dwight declared, because the nation had a special role in bringing the kingdom of God to earth. The land had often been preserved by God, for example, during the wars with the French and Indians and the War of Independence with Britain. It had grown physically and spiritually after the Revolutionary War. Not only was religion purer in the United States, but physical health was better, and there was a more just distribution of wealth.

Dwight said that new signs indicated the beginning of a new age. These signs included the admission of Jews to citizenships in many countries, the prosperous state of foreign missions, the antislavery movement, the decline of Islam, and the great calamities that had befallen the Roman Catholic states of western Europe. The kingdom of God would come to earth, Dwight believed, through revival among Christian people and by the spread of the American system of religious and political liberty throughout the world. God's means for converting mankind was the United States of America. Dwight's attempt to counter the French threat against Christianity led him to advocate his own version of civil religion, which invested his own land with apocalyptic significance. The tendency to identify the state with God's purpose has proven to be a most unfortunate legacy of the revolutionary age. Nationalism, when supported by science, liberalism, and socialism has been a potent challenge to the church in the modern era.

Appendix

READINGS FROM PRIMARY SOURCES

NO. 1—THE FORMULA OF CONCORD

EPITOME OF THE ARTICLES

touching which

CONTROVERSIES

have arisen among the divines of the Augsburg Confession, which in the following restatement have been in godly wise, according to the express word of God, set forth and reconciled.

OF THE COMPENDIOUS RULE AND NORM,

according to which all dogmas ought to be judged, and all controversies which have arisen ought to be piously set forth and settled.

I. We believe, confess, and teach that the only rule and norm, according to which all dogmas and all doctors ought to be esteemed and judged, is no other than the prophetic and apostolic writings both of the Old and of the New Testaments, as it is written (Psalm cxix. 105 . . . [and] Gal. 1. 8). . . .

But other writings, whether of the fathers or the moderns, . . . are in nowise to be equalled to the Holy Scriptures, but are all to be esteemed inferior to them, so that they be not otherwise received than in the rank of witnesses, to show what doctrine was taught after the Apostles' times also, and in what parts of the world that more sound doctrine of the Prophets and Apostles has been preserved.

II. And inasmuch as . . . false teachers and heretics arose, against whom in the primitive Church symbols were composed, that is to say, brief and explicit confessions, which contained the unanimous consent of the Catholic Christian faith, and the confession of the orthodox and true Church (such as are the APOSTLES', the NICENE, and the ATHANASIAN CREEDS): we publicly profess that we embrace them, and reject all heresies and all dogmas which have ever been brought into the Church of God contrary to their decision.

III. And as concerns the schisms in matters of faith, which have come to pass in our times, we judge the unanimous consent and declaration of our Christian faith, especially against the papacy and its idolatrous rites and superstitions, and against other sects, to be the Symbol of our own age, called the First, Unaltered AUGSBURG CONFESSION, which in the year 1530 was exhibited to the Emperor Charles the Fifth at the Diet of the Empire; and likewise the Apology [of the Augsburg Confession]; and the SMALCALD ARTICLES drawn up in the year 1537, and approved by the subscription of the principal divines of that time.

And inasmuch as this matter of religion appertains also to the laity, as they are called, and their eternal salvation is at stake, we publicly profess that we also receive DR. LUTHER'S SMALLER and LARGER CATECHISMS . . . in which all those things are briefly comprehended which in the Holy Scripture are treated more at length, and the knowledge of which is necessary to a Christian man for his eternal salvation.

To these principles, as set forth a little above, every religious doctrine ought to be conformed; and, if any thing is discovered to be contrary to them, that is to be rejected and condemned, as being at variance with the unanimous declaration of our faith. . . .

But the other symbols and other writings, of which we made mention a little while ago, do not possess the authority of a judge—for this dignity belongs to Holy Scripture alone; but merely give testimony to our religion, and set it forth to show in what manner from time to time the Holy Scriptures have been understood and explained in the Church of God by the doctors who then lived, as respects controverted articles, and by what arguments, dogmas at variance with the Holy Scriptures have been rejected and condemned.

ART I.
CONCERNING ORIGINAL SIN
STATEMENT OF THE CONTROVERSY

Whether Original Sin is properly and without any distinction the very nature, substance, and essence of corrupt man, or at the least the principal and pre-eminent part of his substance, namely, the rational soul itself, considered in its highest degree and in its chief powers? Or whether between the substance, nature, essence, body, and soul of man, even after the fall of mankind on the one hand, and Original Sin on the other hand, there be some distinction, so that the nature itself is one thing, and Original Sin another thing, which adheres in the corrupt nature, and also corrupts the nature?

Affirmative

I. We believe, teach, and confess that there is a distinction between the nature of man itself, not only as man was created of God in the beginning pure and holy and free from sin, but also as we now possess it after our nature has fallen; a distinction, namely, between the nature itself, which even after the fall is and remains God's creature, and Original Sin; and that this difference between nature and Original Sin is as great as between the work of God and the work of the devil.

II. We believe, teach, and confess that this distinction should be maintained with the greatest care, because the dogma that there is no distinction between the nature of fallen man and Original Sin is inconsistent with the chief articles of our faith (of Creation, of Redemption, of Sanctification, and the Resurrection of our flesh), and can not be maintained except by impugning these articles.

For God not only created the body and soul of Adam and Eve before the fall, but has also created our bodies and souls since the fall, although these are now corrupt. And to-day no less God acknowledges our minds and bodies to be His creatures and work; . . . (Job x. 8). . . .

And the Son of God, by a personal union, has assumed this nature, yet without sin; and uniting not other flesh, but our flesh to Himself, hath most closely conjoined it, and in respect of this flesh thus assumed He has truly become our brother; . . . (Heb. ii. 14 . . . 16). . . .

This same human nature of ours (that is His own work) Christ has redeemed, the same (inasmuch as it is His own work) He sanctifies, the same doth He raise from the dead, and with great glory (as being His own work) doth He crown it. But Original Sin He has not created, has not assumed, has not redeemed, doth not sanctify, will not raise again in the elect, nor will ever save and crown with heavenly glory, but in that blessed resurrection it shall be utterly abolished and done away.

From these considerations . . . the distinction between our corrupt nature and the corruption which is implanted in the nature, and through which the nature is corrupt, can be easily discerned.

III. But, on the other hand, we believe, teach, and confess that Original Sin is no trivial corruption, but is so profound a corruption of human nature as to leave nothing sound, nothing uncorrupt in the body or soul of man, or in his mental or bodily powers. . . . How great this evil is . . . can only be discerned by means of the revealed word of God. And we indeed affirm that no one is able to dissever this corruption of the nature from the nature itself, except God alone, which will fully come to pass by means of death in the resurrection unto blessedness. For then that very same nature of ours, which we now bear about, will rise again free from Original Sin, and wholly severed and disjoined from the same, and will enjoy eternal felicity. . . . (Job xix. 26). . . .

ART. II
OF FREE WILL
STATEMENT OF THE CONTROVERSY

Since the will of man is to be considered under a fourfold view [in four dissimilar states]: first, before the fall; secondly, since the fall; thirdly, after regeneration; fourthly, after the resurrection of the body: the chief present inquiry regards the will and powers of man in the second state, what manner of powers since the fall of our first parents he has of himself in spiritual things antecedently to regeneration: whether by his own proper powers, before he has been regenerated by the Spirit of God, he can apply and prepare himself unto the grace of God, and whether he can receive and apprehend the divine grace (which is offered to him through the Holy Ghost in the word and sacraments divinely instituted), or not?

AFFIRMATIVE
. . .

I. . . . the following is our faith, doctrine, and confession, to wit: that the understanding and reason of man in spiritual things are wholly blind, and can understand nothing by their proper powers . . . (1 Cor. ii. 14). . . .

II. We believe, teach, and confess, moreover, that the yet unregenerate will of man is not only averse from God, but has become even hostile to God, so that it only wishes and desires those things, and is delighted with them, which are evil and opposite to the divine will . . . (Gen. viii. 21 . . . Rom. viii. 7) . . . .

Therefore . . . it is impossible . . . that man, who by reason of sin is spiritually dead, should have any faculty of recalling himself into spiritual life . . . (Eph. ii. 5 . . . 2 Cor. iii. 5) . . . .

III. Nevertheless the Holy Spirit effects the conversion of man not without means, but is wont to use for effecting it preaching and the hearing of the Word of God . . . (Rom. i. 16 . . . x. 17) . . . . And without question it is the will of the Lord that His Word should be heard, and that our ears should not be stopped when it is preached (Psa. xcv. 8). With this Word is present the Holy Spirit, who opens the hearts of men, in order that, as Lydia did (Acts xvi. 14), they may diligently attend and thus may be converted by the sole grace and power of the Holy Spirit, whose work, and whose work alone, the conversion of man is. For if the grace of the Holy Spirit is absent, our willing and running, our planting, sowing, and watering, are wholly in vain (Rom. ix. 16; 1 Cor. iii. 7); if, that is, He do not give the increase, as Christ says (John xv. 5): "Without Me ye can do nothing." And, indeed, in these few words Christ denies to free-will all power whatever, and ascribes all to divine grace, "that no one may have whereof he may glory before God" (1 Cor. i. 29; 2 Cor. xii. 5; Jer. ix. 23).

ART. V
OF THE LAW AND THE GOSPEL
STATEMENT OF THE CONTROVERSY

It has been inquired: Whether the Gospel is properly only a preaching of the grace of God, which announces to us the remission of sins, or whether it is also a preaching of repentance, rebuking the sin of unbelief as one which is not rebuked by the Law, but only by the Gospel.

AFFIRMATIVE

. . .

I. We believe, teach, and confess that the distinction of the Law and of the Gospel . . . is to be retained with special diligence in the Church of God, in order that the Word of God . . . may be rightly divided. . . .

III. Wherefore, whatever is found in the Holy Scriptures which convicts of sins, that properly belongs to the preaching of the Law.

IV. The Gospel, on the other hand, we judge to be properly the doctrine which teaches what a man ought to believe who has not satisfied the law of God, and therefore is condemned by the same, to wit: that it behooves him to believe that Jesus Christ has expiated all his sins, and made satisfaction for them, and has obtained remission of sins, righteousness which avails before God, and eternal life without the intervention of any merit of the sinner.

V. But inasmuch as the word *Gospel* is not always used in Holy Scripture in one and the same signification . . . if the term *Gospel* is understood of the whole doctrine of Christ, which he set forth in His ministry, as did also His apostles after Him (in which signification the word is used in Mark i. 15 and Acts xx. 21), it is rightly said and taught that the Gospel is a preaching of repentance and remission of sins.

VI. But when the Law and the Gospel are compared together, as well as Moses himself, the teacher of the Law, and Christ the teacher of the Gospel . . . the Gospel is not a preaching of repentance, convicting of sins, but . . . is properly nothing else than a certain most joyful message and preaching full of consolation, not convicting or terrifying, inasmuch as it comforts the conscience against the terrors of the Law, and bids it look at the merit of Christ alone, and by a most sweet preaching of the grace and favor of God, obtained through Christ, lifts it up again.

VII. But as respects the revelation of sin, the matter stands thus: That veil of Moses is drawn over all men's eyes, so long as they hear only the preaching of the Law, and hear nothing of Christ. Therefore they do not, by the Law, truly come to know their sins, but either become hypocrites, swelling with an opinion of their own righteousness, as were aforetime the Pharisees, or grow desperate in their sins, as did the traitor Judas. On this account Christ took upon him to explain the Law spiritually (Matt. v. 21 sqq.; Rom. vii. 14), and in this manner is the wrath of God revealed from heaven against all sinners (Rom. i. 18), in order that, by perceiving the true meaning of the Law, it may be understood how great is that wrath. And thus at length sinners, being remanded to the Law, truly and rightly come to know their own sins. But such an acknowledgment of sins Moses alone could never have extorted from them.

Although, therefore, this preaching of the passion and death of Christ, the Son of God, is full of severity and terror . . . so that it behooves us to seek the whole of our righteousness in Christ alone:

VIII. Nevertheless, so long as the passion and death of Christ place before the eyes the wrath of God and terrify man, so long they are not properly the preaching of the Gospel, but the teaching of the Law and Moses, and are Christ's strange work, through which He proceeds to his proper office, which is to declare the grace of God, to console and vivify. These things are the peculiar function of the evangelical preaching.

NEGATIVE

. . .

We reject, therefore, as a false and perilous dogma, the assertion that the Gospel is properly a preaching of repentance, rebuking, accusing, and condemning sins, and that it is not solely a preaching of the grace of God. For in this way the Gospel is transformed again into Law, the merit of Christ and the Holy Scriptures are obscured, a true and solid consolation is wrested away from godly souls, and the way is opened to the papal errors and superstitions.

ART. VII
OF THE LORD'S SUPPER

. . .

STATEMENT OF THE CONTROVERSY
Which exists between us and the Sacramentarians in this article

It is asked whether in the Holy Supper the true body and true blood of our Lord Jesus Christ are truly and substantially present, and are distributed with the bread and wine, and are taken with the mouth by all those who use this sacrament . . . in such wise, nevertheless, as that believers derive consolation and life from the Supper of the Lord, but unbelievers take it unto condemnation? The Zwinglians deny this presence and dispensation of the body and blood of Christ in the Holy Supper, but we affirm the same.

For a solid explication of this controversy, it is first to be understood that there are two sorts of sacramentarians. For some are exceedingly gross sacramentarians; these in perspicuous and plain words openly profess that which they think in their heart, to wit: that in the Lord's Supper there is nothing more present than bread and wine, which alone are there distributed and received with the mouth. But others are astute and crafty, and thereby the most harmful of all the sacramentarians; these, when talking of the Lord's Supper, make in part an exceedingly high-sounding use of our mode of speaking, declaring that they too believe in a *true* presence of the *true*, substantial, and living body and blood of Christ in the Holy Supper, which presence and manducation, nevertheless, they say to be spiritual, such as takes place by faith. And yet these latter sacramentarians, under these high-sounding phrases, hide and hold fast the same gross opinion which the former have, to wit: that, besides the bread and wine, there is nothing more present or taken with the mouth in the Lord's Supper. For the term (*spiritualiter*) signifies nothing more to them than the Spirit of Christ or the virtue of the absent body of Christ and His merit, which is present; but they think that the body of Christ itself is in no way whatever present, but is contained above in the highest heaven, and they affirm that it behooves us by the meditations of faith to rise on high and ascend into heaven, and that this body and blood of Christ are to be sought there, and in nowise in union with the bread and wine of the Holy Supper.

AFFIRMATIVE

Confession of the sound doctrine of the Supper
of the Lord against the Sacramentarians

I. We believe, teach, and confess that in the Lord's Supper the body and blood of Christ are truly and substantially present, and that they are truly distributed and taken together with the bread and wine.

II. We believe, teach, and confess that the words of the Testament of Christ are not to be otherwise received than as the words themselves literally sound, so that the bread does not signify the absent body of Christ and the wine the absent blood of Christ, but that on account of the sacramental union the bread and wine are truly the body and blood of Christ.

III. Moreover, as concerns the consecration, we believe, teach, and confess that no human work, not any utterance of the minister of the Church, is the cause of the presence of the body and blood of Christ in the Supper, but that this is to be attributed to the omnipotent power of our Lord Jesus Christ alone.

IV. Nevertheless, we believe, teach, and confess, ... that in the use of the Lord's Supper the words of the institution of Christ are by no means to be omitted, but are to be publicly recited, as it is written (1 Cor. x. 16): "The cup of blessing which we bless, is it not the communion of the blood of Christ?" etc. And this benediction takes place by the recitation of the words of Christ.

V. Now the foundations on which we rest in this controversy with the sacramentarians are the following, which, moreover, Dr. Luther had laid in his Larger Confession concerning the Supper of the Lord:

The first foundation is an article of our Christian faith, to wit: Jesus Christ is true, essential, natural, perfect God and man in unity of person, inseparable and undivided.

Secondly: that the right hand of God is everywhere, and that Christ, in respect of his humanity, is truly and in very deed seated thereat, and therefore as present governs, and has in his hand and under his feet, as the Scripture saith (Eph. i. 22), all things which are in heaven and on earth. At this right hand of God no other man, nor even any angel, but the Son of Mary alone, is seated, whence also he is able to effect those things which we have said.

Thirdly: that the Word of God is not false or deceiving.

Fourthly: that God knows and has in his power various modes in which he can be any where, and is not confined to that single one which philosophers are wont to call local or circumscribed.

VI. We believe, teach, and confess that the body and blood of Christ are taken with the bread and wine, not only spiritually through faith, but also by the mouth, nevertheless not Capernaitically, but after a spiritual and heavenly manner, by reason of the sacramental union. For to this the words of Christ clearly bear witness, in which He enjoins us to take, to eat, to drink; and that this was done by the Apostles the Scripture makes mention, saying (Mark xiv. 23): "And they all drank of it." And Paul says: "The bread which we break is the communion of the body of Christ;" that is, he that eats this bread eats the body of Christ. To the same with great consent do the chief of the most ancient doctors of the Church, Chrysostom, Cyprian, Leo the First, Gregory, Ambrose, Augustine, bear witness.

VII. We believe, teach, and confess that not only true believers in Christ, and such as worthily approach the Supper of the Lord, but also the unworthy and unbelieving receive the true body and blood of Christ; and such wise, nevertheless, that they derive thence neither consolation nor life, but rather so as that receiving turns to their judgment and condemnation, unless they be converted and repent (1 Cor. xi. 27, 29). . . .

VIII. We believe, teach, and confess that there is one kind only of unworthy guests: they are those only who do not believe. Of these it is written (John iii. 18): "He that believeth not is condemned already." And this judgment is enhanced and aggravated by an unworthy use of the holy Supper (1 Cor. xi. 29).

IX. We believe, teach, and confess that no true believer, so long as he retains a living faith, receives the Holy Supper of the Lord unto condemnation, however much weakness of faith he may labor under. For the Lord's Supper has been chiefly instituted for the sake of the weak in faith, who nevertheless are penitent, that from it they may derive true consolation and a strengthening of their weak faith (Matt. ix. 12; xi. 5, 28).

X. We believe, teach, and confess that the whole worthiness of the guests at this heavenly Supper consists alone in the most holy obedience and most perfect merit of Christ. And this we apply to ourselves by true faith, and are rendered certain of the application of this merit, and are confirmed in our minds by the sacrament. But in no way does that worthiness depend upon our virtues, or upon our inward or outward preparations.[1]

NO. 2—THE WESTMINSTER SHORTER CATECHISM ...

Question 1. What is the chief end of man?

Answer. Man's chief end is to glorify God, and to enjoy Him forever.

Ques. 2. What rule hath God given to direct us how we may glorify and enjoy Him?

Ans. The Word of God, which is contained in the Scriptures of the Old and New Testaments, is the only rule to direct us how we may glorify and enjoy Him.

Ques. 3. What do the Scriptures principally teach?

Ans. The Scriptures principally teach what man is to believe concerning God, and what duty God requires of man.

Ques. 4. What is GOD?

Ans. God is a Spirit, infinite, eternal, and unchangeable, in His being, wisdom, power, holiness, justice, goodness, and truth. . . .

Ques. 6. How many persons are there in the Godhead?

Ans. There are three persons in the Godhead: the Father, the Son, and the Holy Ghost; and these three are one God, the same in substance, equal in power and glory.

Ques. 7. What are the decrees of God?

Ans. The decrees of God are His eternal purpose according to the counsel of His will, whereby, for His own glory, He hath fore-ordained whatsoever comes to pass. . . .

Ques. 16. Did all mankind fall in Adam's first transgression?

Ans. The covenant being made with Adam, not only for

himself, but for his posterity, all mankind descending from him by ordinary generation, sinned in him, and fell with him, in his first transgression. . . .

Ques. 18. *Wherein consists the sinfulness of that estate whereinto man fell?*

Ans. The sinfulness of that estate whereinto man fell, consists in the guilt of Adam's first sin, the want of original righteousness, and the corruption of his whole nature, which is commonly called original sin; together with all actual transgressions which proceed from it.

Ques. 19. *What is the misery of that estate whereinto man fell?*

Ans. All mankind by their fall lost communion with God, are under His wrath and curse, and so made liable to all the miseries in this life, to death itself, and to the pains of hell forever.

Ques. 20. *Did God leave all mankind to perish in the estate of sin and misery?*

Ans. God, having out of his mere good pleasure, from all eternity, elected some to everlasting life, did enter into a covenant of grace, to deliver them out of the estate of sin and misery, and to bring them into an estate of salvation by a Redeemer.

Ques. 21. *Who is the Redeemer of God's elect?*

Ans. The only Redeemer of God's elect is the Lord Jesus Christ, who being the eternal Son of God became man, and so was, and continueth to be, God and man, in two distinct natures, and one person forever. . . .

Ques. 29. *How are we made partakers of the redemption purchased by Christ?*

Ans. We are made partakers of the redemption purchased by Christ, by the effectual application of it to us by His Holy Spirit. . . .

Ques. 31. *What is effectual calling?*

Ans. Effectual calling is the work of God's Spirit, whereby, convincing us of our sin and misery, enlightening our minds in the knowledge of Christ, and renewing our wills, He doth persuade and enable us to embrace Jesus Christ, freely offered to us in the Gospel.

Ques. 32. *What benefits do they that are effectually called partake of in this life?*

Ans. They that are effectually called do in this life partake of justification, adoption, sanctification, and the several benefits which, in this life, do either accompany or flow from them.

Ques. 33. *What is justification?*

Ans. Justification is an act of God's free grace, wherein He pardoneth all our sins, and accepteth us as righteous in his sight, only for the righteousness of Christ imputed to us, and received by faith alone.

Ques. 34. *What is adoption?*

Ans. Adoption is an act of God's free grace, whereby we are received into the number, and have a right to all the privileges, of the sons of God.

Ques. 35. *What is sanctification?*

Ans. Sanctification is the work of God's free grace, whereby we are renewed in the whole man after the image of God, and are enabled more and more to die into sin, and live unto righteousness.

Ques. 36. *What are the benefits which in this life do accompany or flow from justification, adoption, and sanctification?*

Ans. The benefits which in this life do accompany or flow from justification, adoption, and sanctification, are, assurance of God's love, peace of conscience, joy in the Holy Ghost, increase of grace, and perseverance therein to the end.

Ques. 37. *What benefits do believers receive from Christ at death?*

Ans. The souls of believers are, at their death, made perfect in holiness, and do immediately pass into glory; and their bodies, being still united to Christ, do rest in their graves till the resurrection.

Ques. 38. *What benefits do believers receive from Christ at the resurrection?*

Ans. At the resurrection, believers being raised up in glory, shall be openly acknowledged and acquitted in the day of judgment, and made perfectly blessed in the full enjoying of God to all eternity....

Ques. 85. *What doth God require of us, that we may escape His wrath and curse, due to us for sin?*

Ans. To escape the wrath and curse of God, due to us for sin, God requireth of us faith in Jesus Christ, repentance unto life, with the diligent use of all the outward means whereby Christ communicateth to us the benefits of redemption.

Ques. 86. *What is faith in Jesus Christ?*

Ans. Faith in Jesus Christ is a saving grace, whereby we receive and rest upon Him alone for salvation, as He is offered to us in the Gospel.

Ques. 87. *What is repentance unto life?*

Ans. Repentance unto life is a saving grace, whereby a sinner, out of a true sense of his sin, and apprehension of the mercy of God in Christ, doth, with grief and hatred of his sin, turn from it unto God, with full purpose of, and endeavor after, new obedience. . . .

Ques. 91. *How do the sacraments become effectual means of salvation?*

Ans. The sacraments become effectual means of salvation, not from any virtue in them, or in him that doth administer them, but only by the blessing of Christ, and the working of His Spirit in them that by faith receive them.

Ques. 92. *What is a sacrament?*

Ans. A sacrament is a holy ordinance instituted by Christ; wherein, by sensible signs, Christ and the benefits of the new covenant are represented, sealed, and applied to believers.

Ques. 93. *Which are the sacraments of the New Testament?*

Ans. The sacraments of the New Testament are Baptism and the Lord's Supper.[2]

NO. 3—A SERMON BY JOHN WESLEY

Justification by Faith

> *To him that worketh not, but believeth on Him that justifieth the ungodly, his faith is counted for righteousness.* Rom. 4:5

1. How a sinner may be justified before God, the Lord and Judge of all, is a question of no common importance to every child of man. It contains the foundation of all our hope, inasmuch as while we are at enmity with God, there can be no true peace, no solid joy, either in time or in eternity. What peace can there be, while our own heart condemns us; and much more, He that is "greater than our heart, and knoweth all things?" What solid joy, either in this world or that to come, while "the wrath of God abideth on us?" . . .

3. In order to do justice, as far as in me lies, to the vast importance of the subject, . . . I shall endeavour to show.

First, What is the general ground of this whole doctrine of justification;

Secondly, What justification is;

Thirdly, Who they are that are justified; and,

Fourthly, On what terms they are justified.

I. I am first to show what is the general ground of this whole doctrine of justification. . . .

4. Such then was the state of man in paradise. By the free, unmerited love of God he was holy and happy, he knew, loved, enjoyed God, which is, in substance, life everlasting. And in this life of love he was to continue for ever, if he continued to obey God in all things; but if he disobeyed Him in any, he was to forfeit all. "In that day," said God, "thou shalt surely die."

5. Man did disobey God. He "ate of the tree, of which God commanded him, saying, Thou shalt not eat of it." And in that day he was condemned by the righteous judgment of God. . . .

7. In this state we were, even all mankind, when "God so loved the world, that He gave His only begotten Son, to the end we might not perish, but have everlasting life." In the fulness of time He was made man, another common Head of mankind, a second general parent and representative of the whole human race. And as such it was that "He bore our griefs," "the Lord laying upon Him the iniquities of us all." . . . And by that one oblation of himself, once offered, He hath redeemed me and all mankind; having thereby "made a full, perfect, and sufficient sacrifice and satisfaction for the sins of the whole world." . . .

9. This, therefore, is the general ground of the whole doctrine of justification. By the sin of the first Adam, who was not only the father, but likewise the representative, of us all, we all fell short of the favour of God; . . . . Even so, by the sacrifice for sin made by the second Adam, as the representative of us all, God is so far reconciled to all the world, that He hath given them a new covenant; the plain condition whereof being once fulfilled, "there is no more condemnation" for us, but "we are justified freely by His grace, through the redemption that is in Jesus Christ."

II. 1. But what is it to be *justified*? What is *justification*? This was the second thing which I proposed to show. And it is evident, from what has been already observed, that it is not the being made actually just and righteous. This is *sanctification* . . . a distinct gift of God, and of a totally different nature. The one implies, what God does for us through His Son; the other, what he works in us by His Spirit. So that, although some rare instances may be found wherein the term *justified* or *justification* is used in so wide a sense as to include *sanctification* also; yet, in general use, they are sufficiently distinguished from each other, both by St. Paul and the other inspired writers. . . .

5. The plain scriptural notion of justification is pardon, the forgiveness of sins. It is that act of God the Father, whereby, for the sake of the propitiation made by the blood of His Son, he "showeth forth His righteousness (or mercy) by the remission of the sins that are past." This is the easy, natural account of it given by St. Paul, throughout this whole epistle. . . . Thus, in the next verses but one to the text, "Blessed are they," saith he, "whose iniquities are forgiven, and whose sins are covered: blessed is the man to whom the Lord will not impute sin." . . .

III. 1. But this is the third thing which was to be considered, namely, Who are they that are justified? And the apostle tells us expressly: . . . the ungodly of every kind and degree; and none but the ungodly. As "they that are righteous need no repentance," so they need no forgiveness. . . . It is our *unrighteousness* to which the pardoning God is *merciful:* it is our iniquity which he "remembereth no more." . . .

IV. 1. But on what terms then is he justified, who is altogether *ungodly,* and till that time *worketh not?* On one alone; which is faith: he "believeth in Him that justifieth the ungodly." And "he that believeth is not condemned;" yea, he is "passed from death unto life." . . .

2. Faith in general is a divine, supernatural . . . *evidence* or *conviction,* "of things not seen," not discoverable by our bodily senses, as being either past, future, or spiritual. Justifying faith implies, not only a divine evidence or conviction that "God was in Christ, reconciling the world unto himself;" but a sure trust and confidence that Christ died for *my* sins, that he loved *me,* and gave himself for *me.* And at what time soever a sinner thus believes, be it in early childhood in the strength of his years, or when he is old and hoary-headed, God justifieth that ungodly one: God, for the sake of His Son, pardoneth and absolveth him who had in him, till then, no good thing. . . .

5. Faith, therefore, is the *necessary* condition of justification; yea, and the *only necessary* condition thereof. This is the second point carefully to be observed; that, the very moment God giveth faith (for *it is the gift of God*) to the "ungodly" that "worketh not," that "faith is counted to him for righteousness." He hath no righteousness at all, antecedent to this; not so much as negative righteousness, or innocence. But "faith is imputed to him for righteousness" the very moment that he believeth. . . .

8. One reason, however, we may humbly conceive, of God's fixing this condition of justification, "If thou believest in the Lord Jesus Christ, thou shalt be saved," was to *hide pride from man*. . . . He must come as a *mere sinner* inwardly and outwardly, self-destroyed and self-condemned, bringing nothing to God but ungodliness only, pleading nothing of his own but sin and misery. Thus it is, and thus alone, when his *mouth is stopped,* and he stands utterly *guilty before* God, that he can *look unto Jesus,* as the whole and sole *propitiation for his sins.* Thus only can he be *found in Him,* and receive the "righteousness which is of God by faith."

9. Thou ungodly one, who hearest or readest these words! thou vile, helpless, miserable sinner! I charge thee before God, the Judge of all, go straight unto Him, with all thy ungodliness. . . . Plead thou no works, no righteousness of thine own! no humility, contrition, sincerity! In nowise. That were, in very deed, to deny the Lord that bought thee. No: plead thou singly the blood of the covenant, the ransom paid for thy proud, stubborn, sinful soul. . . . Oh, come quickly! believe in the Lord Jesus, and thou, even thou, art reconciled to God.[3]

Suggestions for Further Reading

Among the useful reference works for the church in the period 1600—1800 are *The New Catholic Encyclopedia*, 15 vols. (New York: McGraw Hill Book Co., 1967); *The New International Dictionary of the Christian Church* (Grand Rapids, Mich.: Zondervan Pub. Co., 1974); *The New Schaff-Herzog Encyclopedia of Religious Knowledge*, 12 vols. (New York: Funk & Wagnalls, 1908—12); and *The New Cambridge Modern History*, vols. IV, V, VII, VIII (Cambridge, England: University Press, 1957—70).

The surveys of church history that are helpful for this period include C. R. Cragg, *The Church and the Age of Reason: 1648—1789* (Baltimore: Penguin Books Ltd., 1960); Harold J. Grimm, *The Reformation Era: 1500—1650* (New York: The Macmillan Company, 1965); Kenneth Scott Latourette, *A History of Christianity, 1500—1975* (New York: Harper & Row Pub., 1975); Clyde L. Manschreck, *A History of Christianity in the World* (Englewood Cliffs, New Jersey: Prentice-Hall, Inc., 1974); John T. McNeill, *Modern Christian Movements* (New York: Harper & Row, Publishers, 1968); Stephen Neill, *A History of Christian Missions* (Baltimore: Penguin Books Ltd., 1964); and James Hastings Nichols, *History of Christianity: 1650—1950* (New York: The Ronald Press Company, 1956).

The following books would also help an individual understand the theology of the age of orthodoxy: Bengt Hagglund, *History of Theology*, tr. Gene J. Lund (St. Louis: Concordia Publishing House, 1968); Heinrich Heppe, *Reformed Dogmatics* (London: Allen & Unwin, Ltd., 1950); and Robert D. Preus, *The Theology of Post-Reformation Lutheranism*, 2 vols. (St. Louis: Concordia Publishing House, 1970—72).

Original source readings can be found in Clyde L. Manschreck, *A History of Christianity: Readings in the History of the Church from the Reformation to the Present* (Englewood Cliffs, New Jersey: Prentice-Hall, Inc., 1964), and Frank E. Manuel, ed., *The Enlightenment* (Englewood Cliffs, New Jersey: Prentice-Hall, Inc., 1965).

An excellent edition of Spener's most important book is Philipp Jacob Spener, *Pia Desideria*, trans. Theodore G. Tappert (Philadelphia: Fortress Press, 1964).

Other works that help the student appreciate Pietism and its leading exponent in the English speaking world are Dale Brown, *Understanding Pietism* (Grand Rapids, Mich.: Wm. B. Eerdmans Publishing Company, 1978); Donald F. Durnbaugh, *The Believers' Church* (New York: The Macmillan Company, 1968); Albert C. Outler, *John Wesley* (New York: Oxford University Press, 1964); and Martin Schmidt, *John Wesley: Theological Biography* (New York: Abingdon Press, 1963).

To set the problems of the church in the context of all facets of 17th- and 18th-century life these works are most helpful: R. W. Harris, *Absolutism and Enlightenment: 1660—1789* (London: Blandford Press, 1967); A. Lloyd Moote, *The Seventeenth Century: Europe in Ferment* (Lexington, Mass.: D. C. Heath & Company, 1970); David Ogg, *Europe of the Ancien Regime, 1715—1783* (London: Collins, 1965); George Rude, *Revolutionary Europe, 1783—1815* (New York: Harper & Row, Publishers, 1964); and R. J. White, *Europe in the Eighteenth Century: 1660—1789* (London: Blandford Press, 1967).

Also suggested for further reading: The Canons of the Synod of Dort (or Dordrecht), in *The Creeds of Christendom*, III, ed. Philip Schaff (New York: Harper and Bros., 1877), 581—585; The Declaration of Independence of the United States; Isaac Newton, *The Mathematical Principles of Natural Philosophy*, II, (London: H. D. Symonds, 1803), 160—162; Jean Jacques Rousseau, *The Social Contract*, in *Famous Utopias* (New York: Tudor Publishing Co., 1901), pp. 3—4, 6—7, 13—15, 89—91.

Notes

CHAPTER 1

1. The followers of John Calvin were known in various countries of Europe as the Reformed Church or Calvinists.
2. Often these statements are suggested by the use of the acronym TULIP.
3. The *Variata* is the 1540 edition of the Augsburg Confession, which was favored by the Calvinists because it allowed sufficient latitude to include their beliefs, especially on the doctrine of Holy Communion.
4. Seven electors chose the Holy Roman Emperor. Three of these (the archbishops of Mainz, Trier and Cologne) were churchmen; the others were secular rulers.

CHAPTER 2

1. Robert D. Preus, *The Theology of Post-Reformation Lutheranism*, (St. Louis: Concordia Publishing House, 1970), I, 62.
2. Perry Miller, *The New England Mind: The Seventeenth Century* (Cambridge, Mass.: Harvard University Press, 1937), p. 102.
3. Bengt Hagglund, *History of Theology*, tr. Gene J. Lund (St. Louis: Concordia Publishing House, 1968), p. 302.
4. *Devotions and Prayers of Johann Arndt*, selected and translated by John J. Stoudt (Grand Rapids, Mich.: Baker Book House, 1958), pp. 62—63.

CHAPTER 3

1. Cotton Mather as quoted in John T. McNeill, *Modern Christian Movements* (Philadelphia: The Westminster Press, 1954), p. 74.
2. *The Journal of the Rev. John Wesley, A. M.*, vol. I, ed. Nehemiah Curnock (London: The Epworth Press, 1912), p. 475—476.
3. *Ibid.*, vol. III, p. 14.
4. *Ibid.*, p. 100.

CHAPTER 4

1. *Memoirs of Augustus Hermann Francke*, prepared for the American Sunday School Union, and revised by the Committee of Publication (Philadelphia: American Sunday School Union, 1831), pp. 67—70.

APPENDIX

1. *The Creeds of Christendom*, III, ed. Philip Schaff (New York: Harper & Bros., 1877), 93—142.
2. *Ibid.*, pp. 676—696.
3. *Sermons by the Rev. John Wesley, A.M.*, I, ed. W. P. Harrison (Nashville, Tenn.: Publishing House of the M. E. Church, South, 1894), 103—116.

Index

By DAVID LUMPP